FastCourse Microsoft® Excel 2010:
LEVEL 3 of 3

SANDRA RITTMAN
Long Beach City College

LABYRINTH
LEARNING™

El Sobrante, CA

FastCourse Microsoft Excel 2010: Level 3
by Sandra Rittman

LABYRINTH
LEARNING™

Labyrinth Learning
P.O. Box 20818
El Sobrante, California 24820
800.522.9746
On the web at lablearning.com

President:
Brian Favro

Product Development Manager:
Jason Favro

Managing Editor:
Laura Popelka

Production Manager:
Rad Proctor

eLearning Production Manager:
Arl S. Nadel

Editorial/Production Team:
Pamela Beveridge, Belinda Breyer,
Everett Cowan, Alec Fehl, Sandy Jones,
Judy Mardar, PMG Media

Indexing: Joanne Sprott

Interior Design:
Mark Ong, Side-by-Side Studios

Cover Design:
Words At Work

ITEM: 1-59136-327-6
ISBN-13: 978-1-59136-327-9

Manufactured in the United States of America.

10 9 8 7 6 5 4 3 2

Table of Contents

Notes

LESSON 1
Creating PivotTables and Macros

Excel has many features to help you perform sophisticated data analyses. In this lesson, you will arrange your data with simple drag-and-drop commands and have Excel automatically create summary formulas in the rows and columns. You also will create PivotTables and PivotCharts. Many Excel workbooks are used on a recurring basis, such as monthly expense accounts, sales forecasts, and various lists. Often, the same tasks are performed in these workbooks over and over. Excel allows you to create macros to automate repetitive tasks. In addition, Excel lets you assign macros to shortcut keys, buttons on the Quick Access toolbar, and custom buttons or other graphics in a worksheet.

LEARNING OBJECTIVES

After studying this lesson, you will be able to:

- Create PivotTables and change their fields
- Create PivotCharts from PivotTable or worksheet data
- Set macro security to protect workbook data
- Record and run macros to automate tasks
- Add custom task buttons to worksheets

LESSON TIMING

- Concepts/Hands-On: 2 hrs 00 min
- Concepts Review: 15 min
- Total: 2 hrs 15 min

CASE STUDY: SIMPLIFYING REPETITIVE TASKS

Raritan Clinic East, an incorporated medical practice that serves a patient community ranging in ages from newborn to 18 years, is planning to construct a pediatric oncology facility. A companion facility will provide temporary housing to physicians specializing in ground-breaking cancer treatments and long-term housing for family members of patients. Sandra Chavez-Hall is the chief development officer for the clinic's foundation. She coordinates a fundraising campaign and will use PivotTables and PivotCharts to analyze the contributions by various criteria. She also maintains a contributions-to-date summary report and uses macros to record the steps used in sorting the data.

Creating PivotTables

PivotTables are powerful data analysis tools. They let you summarize data in various ways and instantly change the view you use. You can create normal Excel lists and tables to sort and filter data and produce subtotals. A PivotTable not only subtotals groups of related data, but also goes a step further and compares one group to another. Compared with performing similar data analyses on a standard worksheet, PivotTables offer tremendous speed and flexibility.

Arranging the Source Data

You create PivotTables from columns or from a table in an Excel worksheet. The data should contain no blank rows or columns. Converting a list to a table is recommended when records will be added after the PivotTable is created. The additional table data are included automatically when the PivotTable is refreshed or updated. Data in a list are not included automatically. The following examples explain two PivotTables based on the same worksheet list.

	A	B	C	D	E	F
3	Pledge Level	Team Leader	Sponsor Category	Sponsor Name	Year 1	Year 2
4	Level 5	Abbott	Organization Contribution	Accountancy Association	0	15,000
5	Level 4	Faber	Corporate Sponsorship	Accurate Biomedical	10,000	10,000
6	Level 1	Lemus	Federal Government Grant	Admin for Children & Fam	5,129,874	8,075,333
7	Level 3	Faber	Corporate Sponsorship	Alpha Supplies Corp.	125,000	50,000
8	Level 6	Nguyen	Individual Contribution	Andres Padilla	0	500

The worksheet data on which the sample PivotTables are based

PivotTable Example 1

You could sort the preceding table by pledge level or sponsor category; however, you could not easily compare totals for the various pledge levels in each sponsor category. This is where the PivotTable comes into use. A PivotTable can summarize some or all of the data in any number of ways, and it creates grand totals for you. Each column in a PivotTable is a *field*. Examine the PivotTable and notice that the Sponsor Category field from the table is used for the row labels, the Pledge Level field for the column labels, and the Year 2 field for the data area and grand totals. Each row displays the amount given by each sponsor group in the various pledge levels.

This PivotTable summarizes contributions from all sponsor groups.

The amount given by each sponsor group is displayed by pledge level.

Sum of Year 2 Row Labels	Column Labels Level 1	Level 2	Level 3	Level 4	Level 5	Level 6	Grand Total
Corporate Grant		1,425,000.00		0.00			1,425,000.00
Corporate Sponsorship	20,300,000.00	250,000.00	350,000.00	22,500.00	28,750.00		20,951,250.00
Federal Government Grant	47,894,948.00						47,894,948.00
Individual Contribution					4,100.00	2,080.00	6,180.00
Individual Sponsorship	15,000,000.00	2,500,000.00	413,579.00	15,000.00	4,475.00	595.00	17,933,649.00
Local Business Contribution					2,634.00	992.00	3,626.00
Local Government Grant			243,500.00				243,500.00
Medical Center/Large Facility		90,250.00					90,250.00
Medical Ctr Contribution		596,432.00	122,340.00				718,772.00
Organization Contribution			50,000.00	28,000.00	39,050.00	3,160.00	120,210.00
Organized Labor/Union Contribution		700,000.00					700,000.00
Physician Office Contribution			25,000.00	20,000.00	30,500.00		75,500.00
Private Grant		2,000,000.00	0.00				2,000,000.00
State Government Grant	35,077,677.00						35,077,677.00
Grand Total	118,272,625.00	7,561,682.00	1,204,419.00	85,500.00	109,509.00	6,827.00	127,240,562.00

Filter buttons allow you to sort and filter the sponsor groups and pledge levels.

PivotTables automatically total the rows and columns and calculate a grand total.

PivotTable Example 2

Using the same table data, you may view the data differently—in this case, summarized first by pledge level and then by sponsor category. To create this type of view, the PivotTable layout shown in the following illustration contains the Pledge Level and then Sponsor Category fields for row labels, no column labels, and the Year 2 field for the data area and totals.

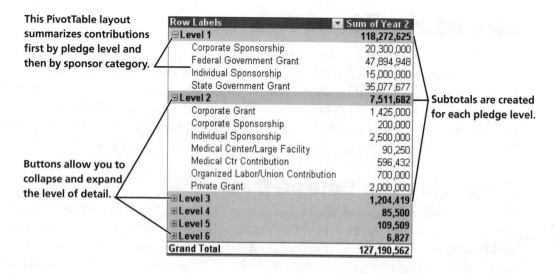

This PivotTable layout summarizes contributions first by pledge level and then by sponsor category.

Subtotals are created for each pledge level.

Buttons allow you to collapse and expand the level of detail.

In this lesson, you will learn how to lay out both of these types of PivotTables and much more.

How PivotTables Work

Each area of the PivotTable plays a role in data organization. The PivotTable Field List task pane displays after you define the worksheet range to be used. The areas of the task pane are explained in the following illustration showing the settings for the preceding PivotTable Example 1.

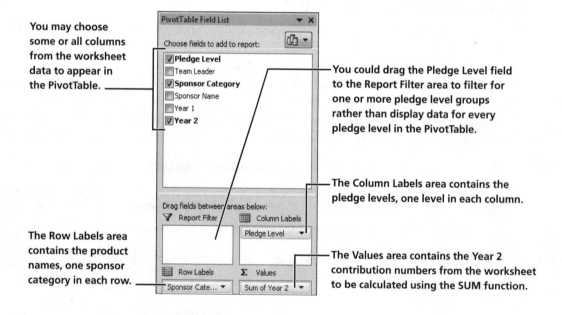

You may choose some or all columns from the worksheet data to appear in the PivotTable.

You could drag the Pledge Level field to the Report Filter area to filter for one or more pledge level groups rather than display data for every pledge level in the PivotTable.

The Column Labels area contains the pledge levels, one level in each column.

The Row Labels area contains the product names, one sponsor category in each row.

The Values area contains the Year 2 contribution numbers from the worksheet to be calculated using the SUM function.

You design a PivotTable by choosing the columns (fields) to be included from the worksheet. Excel initially places all text columns that you choose into the Row Labels area and all selected number columns into the Values area for summing. If this is not your desired layout, you can drag and drop various fields into the correct areas of the task pane. Where you place fields determines how the PivotTable summarizes the data. By choosing different fields or dragging and dropping a field, you may quickly compare data in various ways. You may choose from several functions—such as SUM, COUNT, and AVERAGE—to calculate fields containing values.

Storing Your Exercise Files

Throughout this book, you will be referred to files in your "file storage location." You can store your exercise files on various media, such as on a USB flash drive, in the Documents folder, or to a network drive at a school or company. While some figures may display files on a USB flash drive, it is assumed that you will substitute your own location for that shown in the figures. See Storing Your Exercise Files for additional information on alternative storage media. Storing Your Exercise Files is available on the student web page for this book at labyrinthelab.com/fastcourse_excel10.

Hands-On 1.1: Create PivotTables

Before You Begin: Navigate to the student web page for this book at labyrinthelab.com/fastcourse_excel10 and see the Downloading the Student Exercise Files section of Storing Your Exercise Files for instructions on how to retrieve the student exercise files for this book and to copy them to your file storage location.

1. Start **Excel** and **open** the Sponsors workbook from the Lesson 01 folder in your file storage location.

2. **Maximize** ▫ the window.

3. Select **cell B4**.

4. Choose **Insert→Tables→PivotTable** 🔲 from the Ribbon.

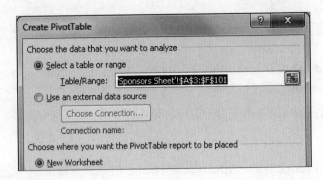

5. Verify the suggested range as shown, notice that the default is to place the PivotTable on a new worksheet, and click **OK**.

6. **Rename** Sheet1 as `PivotTable by Sponsor Category`.

7. Select **cell A1**, which is outside the boundary of the PivotTable outline.

8. Select **cell A3** within the PivotTable placeholder to restore the task pane.

9. Follow these steps to define the PivotTable in the task pane:

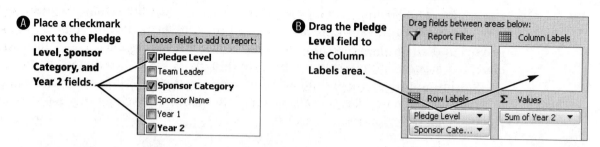

Ⓐ Place a checkmark next to the **Pledge Level, Sponsor Category,** and **Year 2** fields.

Choose fields to add to report:
- ☑ **Pledge Level**
- ☐ Team Leader
- ☑ **Sponsor Category**
- ☐ Sponsor Name
- ☐ Year 1
- ☑ **Year 2**

Ⓑ Drag the **Pledge Level** field to the **Column Labels** area.

Drag fields between areas below:

▽ Report Filter	▦ Column Labels

▦ Row Labels	Σ Values
Pledge Level ▼	Sum of Year 2 ▼
Sponsor Cate... ▼	

	A	B	C	D	E	F	G	H
3	Sum of Year 2	Column Labels ▼						
4	Row Labels ▼	Level 1	Level 2	Level 3	Level 4	Level 5	Level 6	Grand Total
5	Corporate Grant		1425000		0			1425000
6	Corporate Sponsorship	20300000	250000	350000	22500	28750		20951250
7	Federal Government Grant	47894948						47894948
8	Individual Contribution					4100	2080	6180
9	Individual Sponsorship	15000000	2500000	413579	15000	4475	595	17933649
10	Local Business Contribution					2634	992	3626
11	Local Government Grant			243500				243500
12	Medical Center/Large Facility		90250					90250
13	Medical Ctr Contribution		596432	122340				718772
14	Organization Contribution			50000	28000	39050	3160	120210
15	Organized Labor/Union Contribution		700000					700000
16	Physician Office Contribution			25000	20000	30500		75500
17	Private Grant		2000000	0				2000000
18	State Government Grant	35077677						35077677
19	Grand Total	118272625	7561682	1204419	85500	109509	6827	127240562

10. Choose **Options→PivotTable** from the Ribbon, type **BySponsorCategory** in the Pivot-Table name text box, and **tap** Enter.

11. Display the **Sponsors Table** worksheet in the Sponsors workbook.

12. With any table cell selected, choose **Insert→Tables→PivotTable** 🗔 from the Ribbon.

13. Verify that the suggested range is the **Sponsors_Table** and click **OK**.

14. Rename the new sheet as **PivotTable by Pledge Level**.

15. In the PivotTable Field List task pane, place a checkmark next to field names *in this order:* **Pledge Level, Sponsor Category, Year 2**.

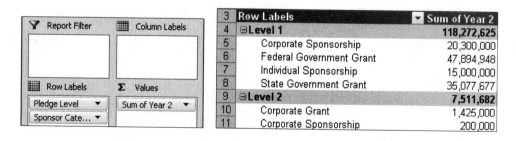

▽ Report Filter	▦ Column Labels

▦ Row Labels	Σ Values
Pledge Level ▼	Sum of Year 2 ▼
Sponsor Cate... ▼	

3	Row Labels ▼	Sum of Year 2
4	⊟ Level 1	118,272,625
5	Corporate Sponsorship	20,300,000
6	Federal Government Grant	47,894,948
7	Individual Sponsorship	15,000,000
8	State Government Grant	35,077,677
9	⊟ Level 2	7,511,682
10	Corporate Grant	1,425,000
11	Corporate Sponsorship	200,000

16. Choose **Options→PivotTable** from the Ribbon, type **By Pledge Level** in the Pivot-Table name text box, and **tap** Enter.

17. Save 💾 the changes to your workbook.

Formatting a PivotTable

Values and subtotals in the PivotTable do not automatically display the formatting from the original worksheet cells. You may set number formatting for a value field. You also may select and format one or more specific cells in the PivotTable. For example, you may align the column labels using commands on the Home tab of the Ribbon. The PivotTable Tools Design contextual tab contains a large selection of PivotTable styles to apply color, shading, and gridlines with one mouse click. The report layout displays in Compact Form by default, or you may choose from two other layouts. The subtotals may be displayed at the top or bottom of each group or hidden.

	A	B
3	Row Labels ▼	Sum of Year 2
4	⊟ Level 1	118,272,625
5	Faber	20,300,000
6	Lemus	82,972,625
7	Weinstein	15,000,000
8	⊟ Level 2	7,561,682
9	Debowski	700,000

The Compact Form report layout
with a PivotTable style applied

	A	B	C
3	Pledge Leve ▼	Team Leader ▼	Sum of Year 2
4	⊟ Level 1	Faber	20,300,000
5		Lemus	82,972,625
6		Weinstein	15,000,000
7	Level 1 Total		118,272,625
8	⊟ Level 2	Debowski	700,000
9		Faber	200,000

The Tabular Form report layout with
filter buttons for each row label field

Hands-On 1.2: Format a PivotTable

1. Display the **PivotTable by Sponsor Category** worksheet in the Sponsors workbook.

2. Select the **range B4:H4** and **right-align** the labels to match the number alignment in their columns.

3. Choose **Design→Layout→Grand Totals menu ▼** from the Ribbon. Experiment by choosing each option and observe its result. Choose **On for Rows and Columns** when you are finished.

4. If necessary, **select** any cell in the PivotTable to redisplay the PivotTable Field List task pane.

5. Follow these steps to format the Year 2 contribution numbers in the PivotTable:

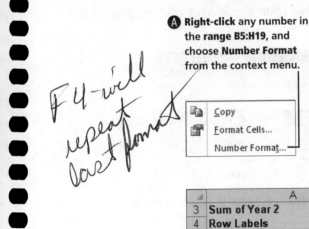

Ⓐ **Right-click** any number in the **range B5:H19**, and choose **Number Format** from the context menu.

Ⓑ Choose the **Number** category, set **0** decimal places, and place a checkmark in the **Use 1000 Separator (,)** box.

Ⓒ Click **OK**.

F4-will repeat last format (handwritten)

	A	B	C	D
3	Sum of Year 2	Column Labels ▼		
4	Row Labels ▼	Level 1	Level 2	Level 3
5	Corporate Grant		1,425,000	
6	Corporate Sponsorship	20,300,000	250,000	350,000
7	Federal Government Grant	47,894,948		

6. Display the **PivotTable by Pledge Level** worksheet.

7. Choose the **Design→PivotTable Styles→More** button, scroll through the available styles, and choose **PivotStyle Medium 9**.

8. Choose **Design→Layout→Report Layout→Show in Outline Form** from the Ribbon.

9. Choose **Design→Layout→Report Layout→Show in Tabular Form** from the Ribbon.

10. Choose **Design→Layout→Report Layout→Show in Compact Form** to return to the original layout.

11. **Save** 🖫 the changes to your workbook.

Changing PivotTable Fields

You may add or remove fields on a PivotTable simply by adding or removing the checkmark next to the field name in the PivotTable Field List task pane. The PivotTable will automatically reconfigure to display the new data. You also may change the order of fields within the row and column areas. One of the most powerful ways of manipulating data is to move a field from the row area to the column area or vice versa. This is called *pivoting the field* (thus the name PivotTable). The display of the data field rotates to give you an entirely different view of your data, as illustrated in the two PivotTables you created in the previous exercise. There, you positioned the Region field to display as columns in the first PivotTable and as rows in the second.

🖱 Hands-On 1.3: Change PivotTable Fields

1. Display the **PivotTable by Pledge Level** worksheet, if necessary.

2. Place a checkmark next to **Year 1** in the task pane to add this field to the PivotTable.

3. **Right-click** any cell in the **Sum of Year 1** column of the PivotTable, and choose **Number Format** from the context menu.

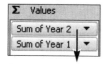

4. In the Format Cells dialog box, choose the **Number** category, set **0** decimal places, place a checkmark in the **Use 1000 Separator (,)** box, and click **OK**.

5. Repeat **steps 3 and 4** to format the **Sum of Year 2** column.

6. **Drag** Sum of Year 2 below Sum of Year 1 in the Values area.

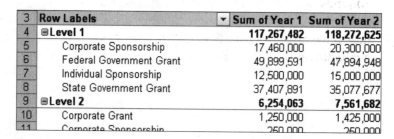

3	Row Labels	Sum of Year 1	Sum of Year 2
4	⊟ **Level 1**	**117,267,482**	**118,272,625**
5	Corporate Sponsorship	17,460,000	20,300,000
6	Federal Government Grant	49,899,591	47,894,948
7	Individual Sponsorship	12,500,000	15,000,000
8	State Government Grant	37,407,891	35,077,677
9	⊟ **Level 2**	**6,254,063**	**7,561,682**
10	Corporate Grant	1,250,000	1,425,000
11	Corporate Sponsorship	250,000	250,000

7. Place a checkmark by the **Sponsor Name** field in the top section of the PivotTable Field List task pane.

4	Row Labels	▼	Sum of Year 1	Sum of Year 2
5	⊟Level 1		117,267,482	118,272,625
6	⊟Corporate Sponsorship		17,460,000	20,300,000
7	Jensen Pharmaceutical		7,500,000	10,000,000
8	Medical Solutions Corp.		5,460,000	4,300,000
9	Open Systems		4,500,000	6,000,000
10	⊟Federal Government Grant		49,899,591	47,894,948
11	Admin for Children & Fam		5,129,874	8,075,333

8. Remove the checkmark by the **Sponsor Category** field and **Sponsor Name** field in the PivotTable Field List task pane.

9. Add a checkmark by the **Team Leader** field.

10. Drag the **Team Leader** field from the Row Labels area to the Column Labels area below the Σ Values field.

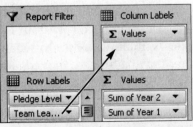

3	Column Labels ▼									Sum of Year 2
4	Sum of Year 1									
5	Row Labels ▼	Abbott	Debowski	Faber	Lemus	Martinez	Nguyen	Park	Weinstein	Abbott
6	⊞Level 1			17,460,000	87,307,482				12,500,000	
7	⊞Level 2		750,000	250,000	2,000,000	754,063			2,500,000	
8	⊞Level 3	50,000		412,000	350,000	207,250			298,333	50,000
9	⊞Level 4	30,000		42,500	50,000	65,000			14,600	28,000
10	⊞Level 5	14,000		20,000		12,500	5,200	2,262	4,325	39,050
11	⊞Level 6	10,646					2,595	1,410	535	3,160
12	Grand Total	104,646	750,000	18,184,500	89,707,482	1,038,813	7,795	3,672	15,317,793	120,210

11. **Undo** 🔄 the pivot you performed in the previous step.

12. **Save** 💾 the changes to your workbook.

Filtering a PivotTable with AutoFilter

You may set the PivotTable to filter, or include, specific items in the data summaries. The totals and subtotals are recalculated for the selected items. The Row Labels and Column Labels headings have an AutoFilter button that displays the same sorting and filtering options that are available on the columns of worksheet lists and tables.

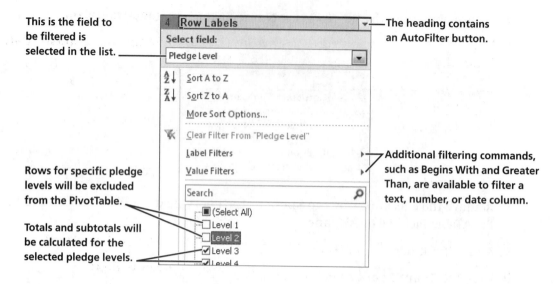

This is the field to be filtered is selected in the list.

The heading contains an AutoFilter button.

Rows for specific pledge levels will be excluded from the PivotTable.

Totals and subtotals will be calculated for the selected pledge levels.

Additional filtering commands, such as Begins With and Greater Than, are available to filter a text, number, or date column.

Filtering PivotTables with Slicers

New to Excel 2010, slicers are menu frames displayed on the worksheet that contain all filtering choices in one field. You can choose items or clear a filter without having to drop down a list. Selected items are highlighted in slicers, making it easy to see which criteria have been applied to the PivotTable filter. Slicer frames may be resized, moved, and formatted with styles for a consistent appearance. Slicers also may be shared in other worksheets of the same workbook for use with multiple PivotTables based on the same data set. Changing the filtering selections in a shared slicer causes all connected PivotTables to update automatically.

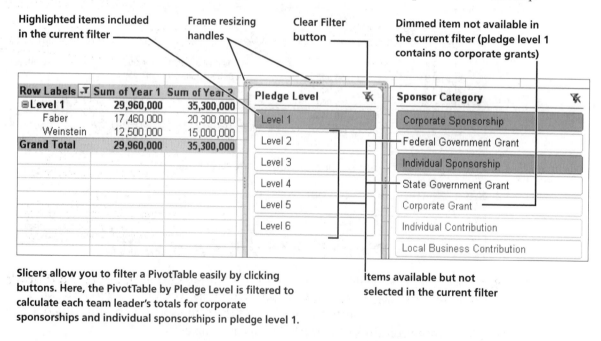

Highlighted items included in the current filter

Frame resizing handles

Clear Filter button

Dimmed item not available in the current filter (pledge level 1 contains no corporate grants)

Items available but not selected in the current filter

Slicers allow you to filter a PivotTable easily by clicking buttons. Here, the PivotTable by Pledge Level is filtered to calculate each team leader's totals for corporate sponsorships and individual sponsorships in pledge level 1.

Hands-On 1.4: Filter a PivotTable with Slicers

1. Display the **PivotTable with Slicers** worksheet in the Sponsors workbook. (**Scroll** to the right in the worksheet tabs to locate the tab, if necessary.)

2. **Select** any cell in the PivotTable to display the PivotTable Tools in the Ribbon, if necessary.

3. Choose **Options→Sort & Filter→Insert Slicer** 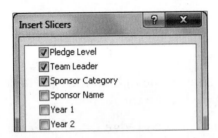 from the Ribbon.

4. Place a checkmark next to the **Pledge Level, Team Leader,** and **Sponsor Category** fields in the Insert Slicers dialog box; click **OK**.

5. Select **cell A1** to hide the PivotTable Field List task pane, if still displayed.

6. Follow these steps to move and resize the Sponsor Category slicer:

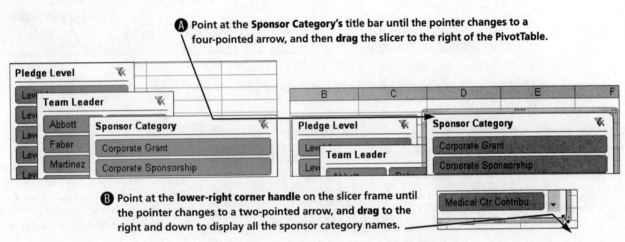

Ⓐ Point at the **Sponsor Category's** title bar until the pointer changes to a four-pointed arrow, and then **drag the slicer to the right of the PivotTable.**

Ⓑ Point at the **lower-right corner handle** on the slicer frame until the pointer changes to a two-pointed arrow, and **drag to the right and down to display all the sponsor category names.**

7. Drag the **Pledge Level** slicer and **Team Leader** slicer to **row 20** as shown.

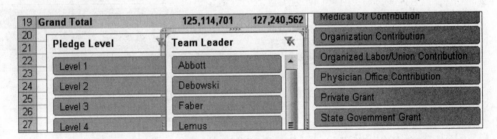

8. Click the **Pledge Level** title to display the slicer's frame, and then **hold down** ⟨Shift⟩ and click on the **Team Leader** title.

9. Choose **Options→Buttons→Columns** 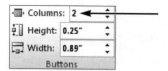 from the Ribbon, and change the number of columns from 1 to **2**.

10. Click the **Sponsor Category** title in the slicer at the right of the PivotTable, choose **Options→Slicer Styles**, and choose any style from the Ribbon.

11. Repeat **step 10** to apply styles of your choice to the **Pledge Level** slicer and **Team Leader** slicer.

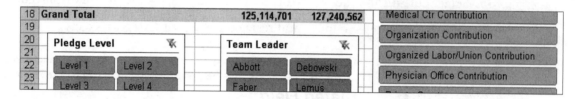

12. Choose **Level 1** in the Pledge Level slicer.

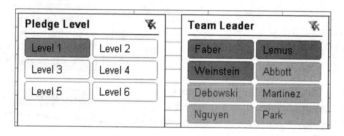

The Team Leader slicer shows that Faber, Lemus, and Weinstein are included in the PivotTable totals. The buttons are dimmed for the other team leaders because they did not solicit any contributions at pledge level 1.

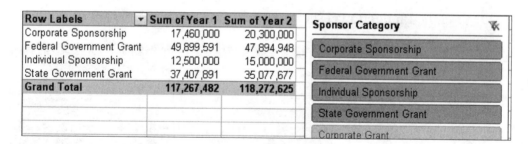

13. Click the **Clear Filter** 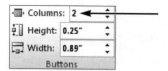 button on the Pledge level slicer to restore all data in the Pivot-Table.

14. Select **Corporate Sponsorship** in the Sponsor Category slicer.

15. **Hold down** ⌃Ctrl and select **Individual Sponsorship**.

16. Experiment by **selecting** and **deselecting** various criteria in the slicers; **clear filters** from all slicers when you are finished.

17. **Save** 💾 the changes to the workbook.

Editing PivotTable Calculations

You are not limited to summing values in a PivotTable, and you may create additional formulas.

Changing the Function for a Values Area Item

By default, the subtotals and grand totals in a PivotTable sum the values in a field. You may use the Summarize Values By command to change the SUM function to a different function, such as AVERAGE, MAX, or COUNT. Not all Excel functions are available by using this command.

Selecting a values column based on Sum of Year 1 and changing the function to AVERAGE changes all columns based on Sum of Year 1.

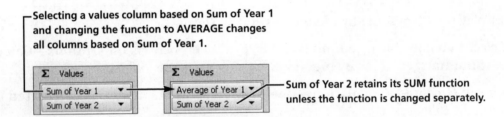

Sum of Year 2 retains its SUM function unless the function is changed separately.

Creating a Calculated Field

Some functions not available with the Summarize Values By command described previously may be typed in the Insert Calculated Field dialog box. A calculated field is a column that you create manually in the PivotTable. This field contains a formula using values from one or more existing fields. For example, the formula could subtract the value in one field from another to find the difference, as shown in the following illustration. You enter the formula once, and Excel displays the formula result in every record of the PivotTable. For accuracy, you should select field names from the list rather than type their names in creating the formula for a calculated field.

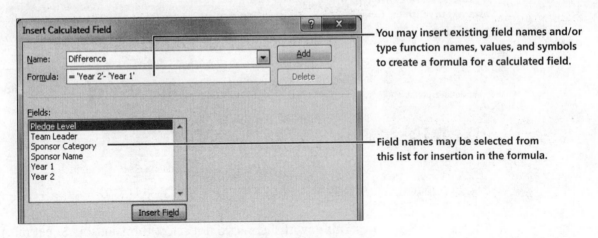

You may insert existing field names and/or type function names, values, and symbols to create a formula for a calculated field.

Field names may be selected from this list for insertion in the formula.

Converting Column Data to a Calculation

The Show Values As command creates formulas using preset options. For example, you can calculate percentages of a total, the difference between values in two columns, a running total, or a ranked order. If you want to display the original column data along with the converted data, simply drag and drop the field name from the field list to the Values area to create a duplicate field.

Refreshing PivotTable Data

FROM THE KEYBOARD

Ctrl+Alt+F5 to refresh all data sources

PivotTables often are created with data from sources external to the Excel workbook containing the PivotTables. For example, the source data may be in another Excel workbook or an Access database. After you change the source data—even if in a worksheet range or table within the same workbook—you must refresh the PivotTables manually. Using the Ribbon, you may refresh just the active PivotTable or all PivotTables in the workbook. You also may set a PivotTable option to refresh data from external sources when the workbook is opened.

Hands-On 1.5: Change PivotTable Calculations

1. Display the **PivotTable by Pledge Level** worksheet.

2. Select a number cell in **column B** of the PivotTable. Then, choose **Options→Calculations→Summarize Values By menu ▼→Average** from the Ribbon.

3. Choose **Options→Calculations→Fields, Items, & Sets menu ▼→Calculated Field** from the Ribbon.

4. Follow these steps to create a calculated field in the Insert Calculated Field dialog box:

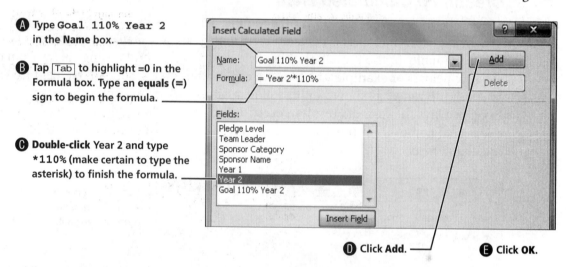

Ⓐ Type Goal 110% Year 2 in the **Name** box.

Ⓑ Tap Tab to highlight =0 in the Formula box. Type an **equals (=)** sign to begin the formula.

Ⓒ **Double-click** Year 2 and type *110% (make certain to type the asterisk) to finish the formula.

Ⓓ Click **Add.**

Ⓔ Click **OK.**

3	Row Labels ▼	Average of Year 1	Sum of Year 2	Sum of Goal 110% Year 2
4	⊟Level 1	13,029,720	118,272,625	130,099,888
5	Faber	5,820,000	20,300,000	22,330,000
6	Lemus	17,461,496	82,972,625	91,269,888
7	Weinstein	12,500,000	15,000,000	16,500,000

5. Display the **Sponsors Table** worksheet. (Do not select the Sponsors Sheet tab.)

6. In **cell F98** for Year 2, change 250,000 to **200000**.

7. Display the **PivotTable by Pledge Level** worksheet.

8. Choose **Options→Data→Refresh menu ▼→Refresh All** from the Ribbon.

9. **Save** 💾 the changes to your workbook.

Creating PivotCharts

A PivotChart presents data from a PivotTable. There are two ways to create a PivotChart.

1. You may chart an existing PivotTable by choosing a chart type from the Insert ribbon as for a normal Excel chart.

2. You may use the PivotChart command to create a PivotTable and PivotChart from the source data at the same time. The chart builds as you choose fields in the PivotTable Field List task pane.

The field(s) in the values area of the PivotTable are displayed as data series in the chart. The row labels in the PivotTable are used as the axis labels in the chart, and the column labels are the data series in the chart legend.

Filtering PivotCharts

The PivotChart may be filtered using the AutoFilter buttons on the chart, AutoFilter buttons on the PivotTable, or slicers added to the worksheet. (See the previous filtering topics in this lesson.) The filtering is applied to the related PivotTable as well.

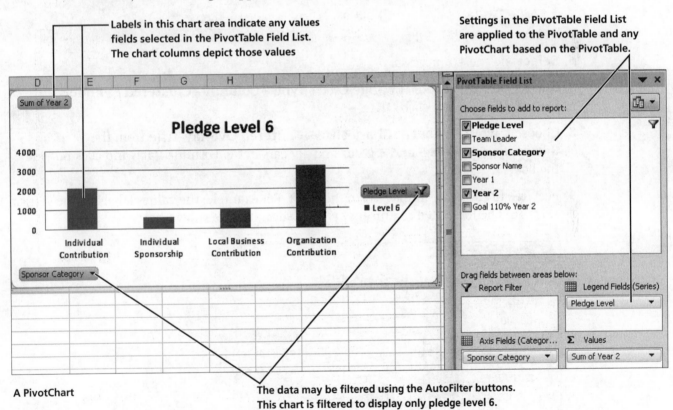

Labels in this chart area indicate any values fields selected in the PivotTable Field List. The chart columns depict those values

Settings in the PivotTable Field List are applied to the PivotTable and any PivotChart based on the PivotTable.

A PivotChart

The data may be filtered using the AutoFilter buttons. This chart is filtered to display only pledge level 6.

Formatting and Printing PivotCharts

You format PivotCharts using the same Ribbon commands as for normal Excel charts. You choose from the same variety of chart styles, including column, line, and pie. You format chart objects just as you would on a normal Excel chart. Some chart formatting, such as data labels, is not preserved after a PivotChart is refreshed. When a PivotChart is selected, the Print command will print only the chart. By first selecting a worksheet cell, you can print both the PivotTable and PivotChart as displayed on the worksheet.

Hands-On 1.6: Create a PivotChart

1. Display the **PivotChart** worksheet of the Sponsors workbook. (**Scroll** to the **right** in the worksheet tabs to locate the tab, if necessary.)

2. **Select** any cell within the PivotTable and choose **Insert→Charts→Column**. Below 2-D Column in the chart types menu, choose **Clustered Column**.

3. **Point** at the chart frame and **drag** the chart just below the PivotTable.

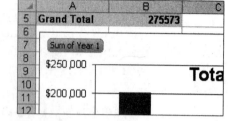

4. Place a checkmark next to **Year 2** in the PivotTable Field List.

5. Follow these steps to filter the PivotChart:

A Choose the **Pledge Level AutoFilter** button at the lower-left corner of the PivotChart.

B **Scroll** down the list.

C Remove the checkmark next to **Level 4**.

- ☐ Level 3
- ☐ Level 4
- ☑ Level 5
- ☑ Level 6

D Click **OK**.

6. **Select** the chart, if necessary.

7. Choose **Design→Type→Change Chart Type→Column→Clustered Cylinder** from the Ribbon and click **OK**.

8. Choose **Layout→Labels→Chart Title→Centered Overlay Title** from the Ribbon, type **Levels 5 and 6** (your text appears in the Formula Bar), and click outside the box.

9. Feel free to add other formatting to the chart. For example, the values labels on the vertical axis could be formatted as Currency with no decimals, as shown here.

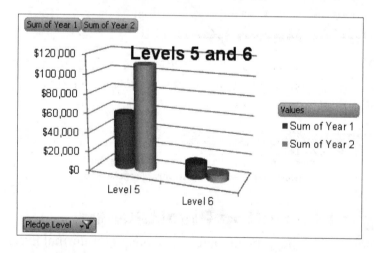

10. **Save** 🖫 the changes.

11. Use ⌃Ctrl + W or the **Close** button shown to close the workbook but leave Excel **open**.

Changing Macro Security

A macro is a recorded set of mouse and keyboard actions that can be played back at any time. Macros are useful for automating routine tasks, especially if those tasks are lengthy. Though macros are a huge timesaver for your frequently used procedures, they also are a prime way to pass viruses to computers. Therefore, be cautious about opening workbooks containing macros that you receive from others.

Security Levels

You change macro security in the Trust Center section within Excel Options. Your setting there is in effect for all Excel workbooks that you open on your computer. The setting is not embedded in any workbooks that you save and share with others. You may choose among four different levels of security in Excel that control whether macros in an opened workbook are available or disabled:

- **Enable all macros**—You are not protected from potentially unsafe macros. This option is not recommended for general use.

- **Disable all macros except digitally signed macros**—This option automatically disables unsigned macros and enables macros from publishers you previously added to the trusted publishers list in the Trust Center. An invisible digital signature or visible signature line may be added to an Excel workbook.

- **Disable all macros with notification**—This is the default option, and it displays a message allowing you to enable macros in the specified workbook if you wish or use the workbook without enabling the macros.

- **Disable all macros without notification**—Only macros in workbooks that you placed in a trusted location of the Trust Center are allowed to run. All other digitally signed and unsigned macros are disabled.

If you have antivirus software installed, the file will be scanned for viruses before it is opened regardless of the security level you set.

Hands-On 1.7: Verify Macro Security

1. Choose **File→Options** 📄 **→Trust Center**. Click the **Trust Center Settings** button and choose the **Macro Settings** category from the left side of the window. Choose **Disable All Macros with Notification** if not already selected.

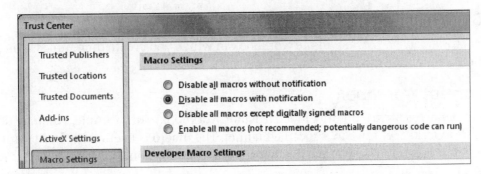

2. Choose the **Message Bar** category from the left side of the window. Verify that the following option is selected: **Show the Message Bar in All Applications When Content, Such As ActiveX and Macros, Has Been Blocked**.

3. Click **OK** twice to exit the Excel Options window.

4. **Open** the Macro Test workbook from the Lesson 01 folder in your file storage location.

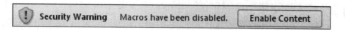

5. Click the **Enable Content** button next to the Security Warning.

6. Click the **Sort by Leader** button.

7. **Close** the workbook without saving changes.

Recording Macros

Excel's macro recording feature saves your keystrokes and the commands you issue for a task. For example, you may record steps to choose page layout options and print a document by clicking the appropriate commands in the Ribbon. You then may play back a recorded macro at a later time. This is similar to using a video camera. You turn it on, press the record button, and stop recording when finished. You may replay the recording as many times as you want. Similarly, macros play back recorded keystrokes and mouse actions.

 After the Record Macro button is clicked in the Status Bar, the Stop Recording button appears.

Naming a Macro

You should name your macros. If you do not, Excel names them Macro1, Macro2, and so on. Name your macros following the same rules that are used for defined names for ranges. Macro names may not contain spaces but may include capital letters or underscores to separate words. For example, you may name a macro FormatTitle or Format_Title.

Recording Macro Steps

Most actions you perform are recorded in the macro. These include mouse actions, choosing Ribbon commands, selecting options in dialog boxes, using cursor keys to navigate the worksheet, and typing text. Any mistakes and corrections you make during recording also are saved in the macro. You may decide not to rerecord the macro, however, if the final result is correct.

Storing Macros

Macros are available only in the workbook in which you create them unless you assign them to the Personal Macro Workbook.

Current Workbook

Some macros are useful only in a particular workbook. For example, you may develop a macro to sort worksheet rows in a specific manner. The macro is useful only in the workbook in which it is created, so you would choose the storage option This Workbook.

Personal Macro Workbook

The Personal.xlsb file is a hidden file that makes its macros available in all open workbooks on your computer system. For example, you may create a macro to format headings with a consistent style to be used in various workbooks. You will assign a macro to the Personal Macro Workbook and delete macros from it in a Skill Builder exercise of this lesson.

Saving a Workbook Containing Macros

If you attempt to save a workbook containing macros using the normal Excel Workbook file format, Excel displays the message "The following features cannot be saved in macro-

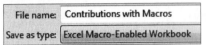

free workbooks: VB Project." Clicking No in the message box displays the Save As dialog box, where you should choose the Excel Macro-Enabled Workbook file format. The file is saved with the extension .xlsm in the file name to indicate that it contains a macro.

 Hands-On 1.8: Record a Macro

1. **Open** the Contributions workbook.

2. Click the **Record Macro** 📷 button on the Status Bar at the bottom-left corner of the window. (**Right-click** the Status Bar and choose **Macro Recording** in the context menu if the button does not display. **Tap** ⌨Esc to hide the context menu.)

3. Follow these steps to name the macro and begin the recording process:

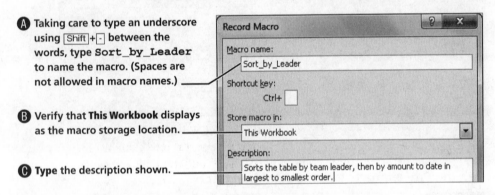

Ⓐ Taking care to type an underscore using ⌨Shift+⌨- between the words, type **Sort_by_Leader** to name the macro. (Spaces are not allowed in macro names.)

Ⓑ Verify that **This Workbook** displays as the macro storage location.

Ⓒ Type the description shown.

4. Click **OK**, and the macro will begin recording your actions.

5. Select **cell B4** in the table.

6. Choose **Data→Sort & Filter→Sort** from the Ribbon.

7. Follow these steps to set the Sort parameters and initiate the Sort:

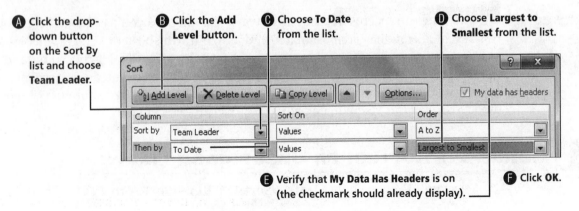

Ⓐ Click the drop-down button on the Sort By list and choose **Team Leader**.

Ⓑ Click the **Add Level** button.

Ⓒ Choose **To Date** from the list.

Ⓓ Choose **Largest to Smallest** from the list.

Ⓔ Verify that **My Data Has Headers** is on (the checkmark should already display).

Ⓕ Click **OK**.

8. Click the **Stop Recording** ■ button on the Status Bar at the bottom-left corner of the window.

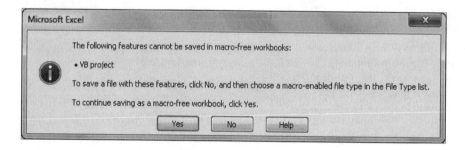

	A	B	C	D	E	F	G
3	Pledge	Team Leader	Sponsor Category	Sponsor Name	Year 1	Year 2	To Date
4	Level 3	Abbott	Organization Contribution	Child Advocate Society	50,000	50,000	100,000
5	Level 4	Abbott	Organization Contribution	Hands Across Foundation	20,000	15,500	35,500
6	Level 4	Abbott	Organization Contribution	Chamber of Commerce	10,000	12,500	22,500
7	Level 5	Abbott	Organization Contribution	Accountancy Association	0	15,000	15,000
8	Level 5	Abbott	Organization Contribution	Business Roundtable	0	15,000	15,000
9	Level 5	Abbott	Organization Contribution	For the Child	5,000	5,000	10,000
10	Level 6	Abbott	Organization Contribution	GEM	5,525	3,160	8,685
11	Level 5	Abbott	Organization Contribution	Nursing Students Assn.	4,000	4,050	8,050
12	Level 5	Abbott	Organization Contribution	Road Warriors Club	5,000	0	5,000
13	Level 6	Abbott	Organization Contribution	UPB Volunteer Program	5,000	0	5,000
14	Level 6	Abbott	Organization Contribution	Fit Kids Club	121	0	121
15	Level 2	Debowski	Organized Labor/Union Contribution	IOEEF	250,000	250,000	500,000
16	Level 2	Debowski	Organized Labor/Union Contribution	Nurses Assn., Local 322	250,000	250,000	500,000

9. Click **Save** 💾.

Microsoft Excel

The following features cannot be saved in macro-free workbooks:

• VB project

To save a file with these features, click No, and then choose a macro-enabled file type in the File Type list.

To continue saving as a macro-free workbook, click Yes.

| Yes | No | Help |

10. Click **No** to display the Save As dialog box.

11. Edit the **File Name** to **Contributions with Macros**.

12. Drop down the Save As type list, choose **Excel Macro-Enabled Workbook**, and click **Save**.

File name: Contributions with Macros

Save as type: Excel Macro-Enabled Workbook

Running Macros

FROM THE KEYBOARD

Alt + F8 to view macros

You may run macros in a variety of ways. The method you use depends on how the macro was assigned. You may create a macro and assign it to a shortcut key, graphic, or Quick Access toolbar button. An unassigned macro must be run by using the Macros command on the Ribbon and selecting a macro. This procedure may be used to run any macro recorded in the current workbook, even if the macro was assigned. The keyboard shortcut Alt + F8 may be used to display the Macro dialog box.

Hands-On 1.9: Run an Unassigned Macro

1. Select **cell D4** and choose **Data→Sort & Filter→Sort A to Z** from the Ribbon.

2. Choose **View→Macros→View Macros** from the Ribbon.

3. Choose the **Sort_by_Leader** macro and click **Run** in the Macro dialog box.

4. **Save** the changes to the workbook.

Assigning Macros

You may run a macro from within the Macro dialog box. However, macros are more accessible if you assign them to shortcut keys, custom buttons or graphics on a worksheet, or buttons on the Quick Access toolbar. You then run the macro by issuing the shortcut key or clicking the object to which the macro is assigned.

Assigning Macros to Shortcut Keys

Excel lets you assign a macro to a shortcut key as you name the macro. You may run the macro simply by using the shortcut key combination. You must use Ctrl or Ctrl + Shift as part of the shortcut key combination. Any shortcut you assign will override an existing Excel command shortcut. For example, you may assign Ctrl + B to a macro, but that combination would no longer choose Bold from the Ribbon.

Hands-On 1.10: Assign a Macro to a Shortcut Key

1. Click the **Record Macro** button on the Status Bar.

2. Follow these steps to name a new macro:

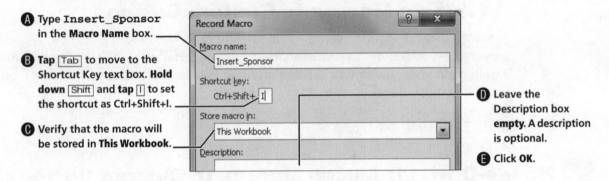

A Type `Insert_Sponsor` in the **Macro Name** box.

B Tap Tab to move to the Shortcut Key text box. **Hold down** Shift and **tap** I to set the shortcut as Ctrl+Shift+I.

C Verify that the macro will be stored in **This Workbook**.

D Leave the Description box empty. A description is optional.

E Click **OK**.

3. Select **cell A4**.

4. Taking care not to select the menu ▾ button, choose **Home→Insert Cells** from the Ribbon.

5. Select the **range A5:G5**, and choose **Home→Clipboard→Format Painter** from the Ribbon.

6. Select **cell A4** to apply the cell formatting from row 5 to the blank row 4.

7. Select **cell A4** again to position the pointer for data entry.

8. Click the **Stop Recording** button on the status bar.

9. Delete the blank **row 4** that you inserted while creating the macro.

10. Use [Ctrl]+[Shift]+[I] to run the Insert_Sponsor macro. (Hold down [Ctrl], then also hold down [Shift], and then tap [I]. Release [Ctrl] and [Shift].)

11. **Add** the following sponsor to the table. **Tap** [Tab] after entering the Year 2 value, and the To Date total will be calculated automatically.

4	Level 6	Weinstein	Individual Contribution	Raul T. Garcia	0	500	500

12. **Run** the Insert_Sponsor macro again and add this sponsor to the table:

4	Level 6	Weinstein	Individual Contribution	Wayne Zobe	0	300	300

13. Choose **View→Macros→View Macros**  from the Ribbon.

14. Choose the **Sort_by_Leader** macro and click **Options** in the Macro dialog box.

15. In the Shortcut Key text box, **press** [Shift], and **tap** [L] to set the shortcut key to Ctrl+Shift+L. Click **OK**.

16. Click **Cancel** to exit the Macro dialog box.

17. Use [Ctrl]+[Shift]+[L] to run the macro.

18. **Save** 🖫 the changes to the workbook.

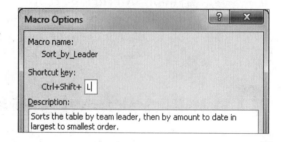

Assigning Macros to Custom Buttons

A macro assigned to a custom button is run whenever the button is clicked. The easiest way to create a custom button is to add a shape, such as a rectangle, to the worksheet. You then assign a macro to the button. You may position custom buttons anywhere in a worksheet. To avoid deleting buttons in error, do not place them in rows or columns that could be deleted in the future. A custom button may also contain a descriptive label to help identify its function or the macro that is assigned to it.

🖱 Hands-On 1.11: Assign Macros to Custom Buttons

1. Choose **Insert→Illustrations→Shapes→Rectangles→Rectangle** ▭ shape tool from the Ribbon.

2. Drag the mouse to draw a button on **cell D1**.

3. Copy and paste the button to cell **E1**.

4. Select the **first button** and type **Insert Sponsor**; do *not* tap [Enter].

5. Select the **second button** and type **Sort by Leader**.

6. **Click** outside the button to deselect it.

7. If necessary, **align** the buttons: Select the first button, use [Shift]+click to select the second button, and choose **Format→Arrange→Align→ Align Top** from the Ribbon.

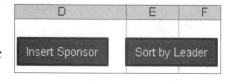

8. **Deselect** the two buttons.

9. **Right-click** the Insert Sponsor button and choose **Assign Macro** from the context menu.

10. In the Assign Macro dialog box, choose **Insert_Sponsor** from the list and click **OK**.

11. Use the preceding steps to assign the **Sort_by_Leader** macro to its button.

12. **Deselect** the button.

13. Click the **Insert Sponsor** button to run the Insert_Sponsor macro. (Deselect the button and select again if the pointer does not display as a hand as you select the button.)

14. Add this sponsor to the new row:

4	Level 3	Abbott	Organization Contribution	Kelsey Foundation	0	50,000	50,000

15. Click the **Sort by Leader** button to run the Sort_by_Leader macro.

16. **Save** 🖫 the changes and **close** the workbook.

Concepts Review

Concepts Review   labyrinthelab.com/fastcourse_excel10

To check your knowledge of the key concepts introduced in this lesson, complete the Concepts Review quiz by going to the URL listed above.

LESSON 2

Using Financial Functions and Data Analysis

Several Excel tools allow you to perform a *what-if analysis* on worksheet data. For example, you might ask, "What if our company obtained a loan for 9 percent rather than 8 percent?" By changing the interest rate used in a formula to various rates, you could see the effect on the monthly loan payment. Excel's built-in financial functions may be used for various types of calculations. In this lesson, you will use the PMT (Payment) function to determine the monthly payment for a business loan and use the FV (Future Value) function to determine the future value of investments. Excel provides other tools to help you find solutions to what-if questions. In this lesson, you will use Goal Seek, Solver, and the Scenario Manager.

LESSON TIMING

- Concepts/Hands-On: 1 hr 15 min
- Concepts Review: 15 min
- Total: 1 hr 30 min

LEARNING OBJECTIVES

After studying this lesson, you will be able to:

- Use the PMT and FV functions to analyze loans and investments
- Adjust one or more variables using the Goal Seek and Solver tools
- Create what-if models in the Scenario Manager

CASE STUDY: ANALYZING A FUNDRAISING CAMPAIGN

Sandra Chavez-Hall coordinates a fundraising campaign to build two new facilities at Raritan Clinic East. The clinic will borrow an initial amount to begin the planning process. Sandra will set up a worksheet that calculates the loan repayment schedule using the PMT function and a variety of input variables. Major funding for the projects will be provided by grants and sponsors. One contribution plan allows corporate and individual sponsors to make monthly payments toward their pledge amounts. These payments will be invested, and Sandra will use the FV function to forecast the total earned. Then she will use Goal Seek, Solver, and Scenario Manager to explore financial scenarios.

Creating Financial Functions

Excel provides more than 50 financial functions that calculate important financial numbers. For example, Excel has basic financial functions for determining monthly payments on loans, the total interest paid on loans, the future value of investments, and other such questions. Excel also has advanced financial functions for calculating depreciation of assets, internal rates of return, and other more advanced business topics.

PMT and FV Functions

The PMT (Payment) and FV (Future Value) functions are the most useful financial functions for the average Excel user. The PMT function calculates the required payment for a loan when you specify the loan amount, interest rate, and number of payments you will make. The FV function calculates the total amount you will have in an investment when you specify the deposit amount, interest rate, and number of deposits.

Financial Function Syntax

You may enter financial functions using the Insert Function dialog box or by typing them. You may use the actual values or cell references in the formulas. Keep in mind that using the cell reference offers more flexibility. For example, you may easily change the number of deposits in an FV function without having to edit the formula. Like all other functions, financial functions have a specific syntax you must follow. The generic format of the PMT and FV functions are shown in the following table.

Function	Syntax
PMT (Payment)	PMT (rate, periods, loan amount)
FV (Future Value)	FV (rate, periods, payment)

Most car loans and fixed-rate mortgages have payment amounts that remain constant throughout the term of the loan. The PMT and FV functions can be used when the payment amount remains constant. The various arguments in the PMT and FV functions are outlined in the following table.

Argument	Description
Periods	This is the number of payments made for a loan or deposits for an investment. Most loans have a monthly payment period, so you should specify the number of months instead of the number of years. For example, use 60 as the number of periods for a five-year auto loan (5 years*12 months per year).
Rate	This is the interest rate for each period of the loan or investment. Although loans are quoted as annual rates, payments usually are made monthly. Therefore, you will need to divide the interest rate by 12 in the formula. For example, a 7 percent annual rate would be expressed as 7%/12.
Payment	This is the amount invested in each period. The payment must be the same for each period.
Loan amount	This is the amount borrowed.
Present value (optional)	This is the starting balance of an investment, such as the current amount in a savings account. You are not required to enter the argument if the starting balance is 0 (zero).
Future value (optional)	This is the balance you wish to have at the end of an investment. You are not required to enter the argument if the balance will be 0 (zero).
Type (optional)	This indicates when the payments are due. You are not required to enter the default argument 0 (zero) if payments are made at the end of the period, such as the last day of each month. Enter 1 if payments are due at the beginning of the period.

Converting Negative Numbers to Positive

Excel treats payments as debits (money you owe), so the PMT and FV functions display the result as a negative number. This is a convention that bankers and other financial professionals use. Placing a minus (–) sign before the cell reference for the loan amount or payment in the formula changes the result to a positive number, which may be more easily understood.

 ## Hands-On 2.1: Use the PMT and FV Functions

1. **Start** Excel and **open** the Fundraising workbook from the Lesson 02 folder in your file storage location.

2. **Maximize** ⬚ the window, if necessary.

3. In the Loan worksheet, select **cell B6** and enter the formula **=B3-B13**.

4. Select **cell B7** and enter **6%** as the interest rate.

5. Select **cell B8** and enter **60** as the number of months.

6. Select **cell B9** and enter the formula **=PMT(B7,B8,B6)**.

7. Select **cell B9**.

8. Click in the **Formula Bar**, position the insertion point after the equals (=) sign in the formula, and **type** a minus (–) sign.

9. Position the insertion point after **cell B7** in the formula and type **/12** to divide the **cell B7** rate by 12, and **complete** the entry.

10. Format **cell B9** in Accounting format with two decimal places.

11. Select **cell B14** and enter the formula **=B9*B8**.

12. Select **cell B10** and enter the formula **=B14-B6**.

13. Select **cell B15** and enter the formula **=B13+B14**.

	A	B
1	Loan Analysis	
2		
3	Phase 1 Site Plan Cost	$700,000.00
4		
5	Loan	
6	Loan Amount	$600,000.00
7	Interest Rate	6.00%
8	Number of Months	60
9	Monthly Payment	$ 11,599.68
10	Total Interest	$ 95,980.86
11		
12	Total Cost	
13	Down Payment	$100,000.00
14	Total Loan Payments	$695,980.86
15	Total Financed Cost	$795,980.86

14. **Save** 🖫 the changes to the workbook.

15. Display the **Investment** worksheet of the Fundraising workbook.

16. Select **cell B5**, and type **0** to indicate that the sponsor will make no initial contribution.

17. Select **cell B7**, and enter **2.5%** for the annual interest rate.

18. Select **cell B8**, and enter **36** for the number of monthly payments.

19. Select **cell B6**, and enter the formula **=B3/B8**.

20. Select **cell B9**.

21. Follow these steps to choose the FV (Future Value) function:

	A	B
1	Invested Contributions	
2		No initial contribution
3	Pledge Amount	$300,000.00
4		
5	Starting Balance	$ -
6	Monthly Contribution	$ 8,333
7	Interest Rate	2.5%
8	Number of Months	36
9	Total Investment	

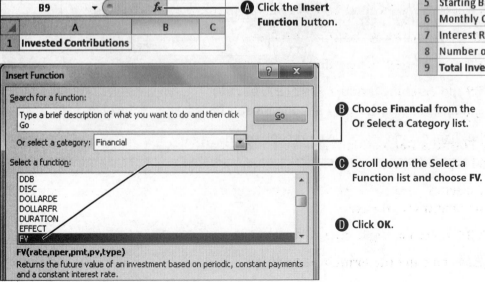

Ⓐ Click the **Insert Function** button.

Ⓑ Choose **Financial** from the Or Select a Category list.

Ⓒ Scroll down the Select a Function list and choose **FV**.

Ⓓ Click **OK**.

FV(rate,nper,pmt,pv,type)
Returns the future value of an investment based on periodic, constant payments and a constant interest rate.

22. Follow these steps to specify the function arguments:

A If necessary, drag the **Function Arguments** dialog box aside so that the range **A1:B9** is visible.

B Click in the **Rate** box, select **cell B7** in the worksheet, and type **/12**. This divides the annual interest rate by 12 months.

C Click in the **Nper** box and select **cell B8** in the worksheet to set the number of payment periods.

D Click in the **Pmt** box. Type a minus (−) sign and click **cell B6** to set the payment amount to a negative value.

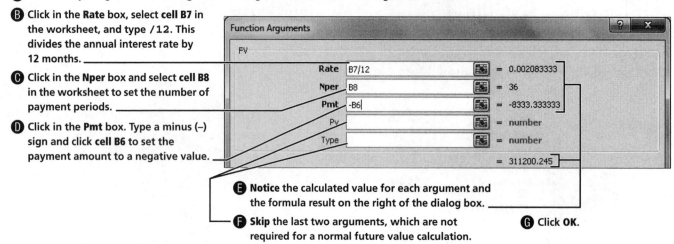

E Notice the calculated value for each argument and the formula result on the right of the dialog box.

F Skip the last two arguments, which are not required for a normal future value calculation.

G Click **OK**.

23. Select **cell E5**, and enter the formula **=E3*25%** for the initial contribution.

24. Copy the **range B6:B9** to the **range E6:E9**.

25. Select **cell E6**, and click in the **Formula Bar**.

26. Making certain to type the **parentheses**, edit the formula to **=(E3−E5)/E8**.

27. Select **cell E9**, and click the **Insert Function** 𝒇𝒙 button at the left of the Formula Bar to display the Insert Function dialog box.

28. Follow these steps to enter optional arguments:

A Click in the **PV** text box, and type **−E5**.

B Click in the **Type** text box, and type **1**.

C Click **OK**.

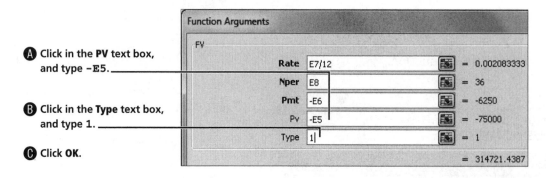

29. Change the number of months to 24 in **cells B8** and **E8**.

30. Save 💾 the changes, and leave the workbook **open**.

Using Data Analysis Tools

Excel provides several tools to perform advanced what-if analyses. Goal Seek is best used when you know the formula answer you want but not the specific value in one cell that would achieve the answer. The Solver sets the values of multiple cells to produce the desired result that you specify for a target cell. You also may set minimum and maximum values for Solver to use in calculations. Scenario Manager saves a model worksheet with various changes to values so that you may compare the scenarios side by side.

Using Goal Seek

With Goal Seek you set a goal for a specific formula result. For example, you will set a monthly payment goal of $10,000 in the Loan worksheet. The goal cell must contain a formula, which is a PMT function in this example. You will instruct Goal Seek to adjust the down payment to achieve the desired monthly payment.

 Hands-On 2.2: Use Goal Seek

1. Display the **Loan** worksheet of the Fundraising workbook.

2. Select **cell B9**.

3. Choose **Data→Data Tools→What-If Analysis** 🔢 →**Goal Seek** from the Ribbon.

4. Follow these steps to set the Goal Seek parameters:

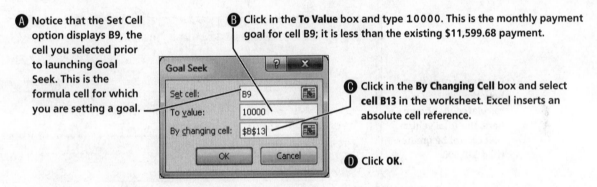

Ⓐ Notice that the Set Cell option displays B9, the cell you selected prior to launching Goal Seek. This is the formula cell for which you are setting a goal.

Ⓑ Click in the **To Value** box and type **10000**. This is the monthly payment goal for cell B9; it is less than the existing $11,599.68 payment.

Ⓒ Click in the **By Changing Cell** box and select **cell B13** in the worksheet. Excel inserts an absolute cell reference.

Ⓓ Click **OK**.

5. Click **Cancel** in the Goal Seek Status dialog box to undo the change to the down payment.

6. Make certain **cell B9** is still selected and choose **Data→Data Tools→What-If Analysis→Goal Seek** from the Ribbon.

7. Type **12000** in the **To Value** box to set the monthly payment goal.

8. Click in the **By Changing Cell** box, and then select **cell B7** (the interest rate cell) in the worksheet.

9. Click **OK**, and the interest rate is changed to 7.42 percent.

10. Move the **Goal Seek Status** dialog box, if necessary, to see **cell B7**.

11. Click **OK** again to confirm the change to the interest rate.

12. **Save** 🖫 the changes.

13. Select **cell B3** and change the **site plan cost** to **$500,000**.

14. Feel free to experiment with Goal Seek. When you are finished, **close** ⊠ the workbook **without** saving the changes.

Using Solver

🔁 Goal Seek is easy to use but is somewhat limited. Goal Seek adjusts only one variable at a time. Excel's Solver tool can solve problems when more than one variable requires adjustment. In fact, you may specify up to two hundred variables, but all variables must appear in a formula related to the objective cell. You may specify a precise objective cell value, as with Goal Seek, or you may specify that Solver determine the Max (maximum) or Min (minimum) value. For example, you may specify a monthly payment of $300 for an auto loan. In addition, Solver lets you specify one or more constraints. Constraints give you extra control by limiting a cell's possible range of values in the suggested solution. You may not set a constraint for any cell that is used in the objective cell's formula. Instead, you must enter the desired value in the appropriate worksheet cell. The new Solver version in Excel 2010 includes a choice of three solving methods. The default GRG Nonlinear method is appropriate for many typical business problems that have a smooth nonlinear solution.

Solver changes the values in these two worksheet cells to meet the specified objective and restraint. In this example, the solution will display an optimum car purchase price and loan interest rate.

A specific value is set for the objective cell, a $300 monthly car payment in this example.

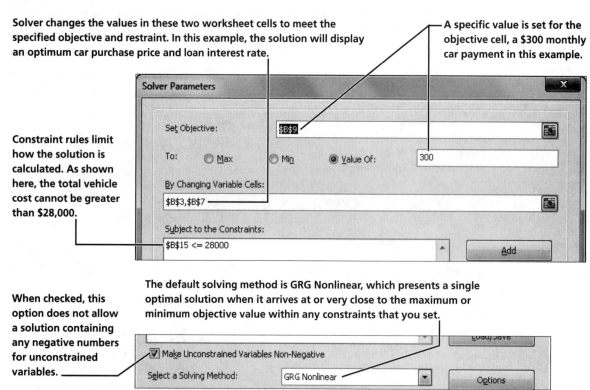

Constraint rules limit how the solution is calculated. As shown here, the total vehicle cost cannot be greater than $28,000.

When checked, this option does not allow a solution containing any negative numbers for unconstrained variables.

The default solving method is GRG Nonlinear, which presents a single optimal solution when it arrives at or very close to the maximum or minimum objective value within any constraints that you set.

Solving for optimum values in two cells based on an objective cell value and a constraint rule

Installing Solver

Solver is not part of the typical Office 2010 installation but is an add-in program. The Solver command displays in an Analysis group on the Data ribbon after installation.

Hands-On 2.3: Use Solver

1. **Open** the Fundraising workbook from the Lesson 02 folder.

2. In the **Loan** worksheet, **reenter** the original value of **6%** in cell B7. Make certain that **cell B3** contains $700,000.00, **cell B8** contains 60, and **cell B13** contains $100,000.00.

3. Choose **Data→Analysis→Solver** ?⇒ from the Ribbon.

4. Follow these steps to set the objective cell value and specify the variable cells:

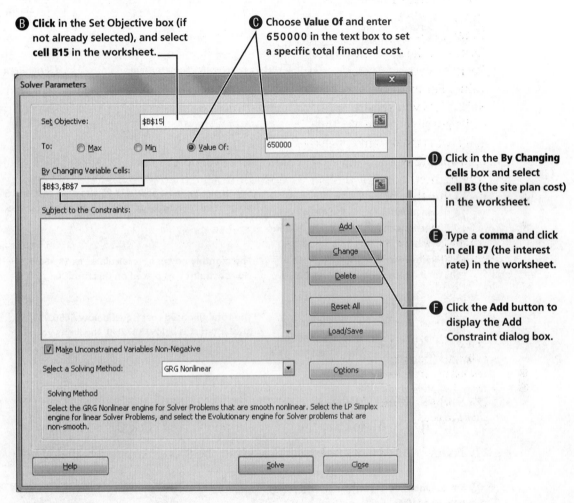

Ⓐ Click the **Reset All** button and click **OK** to confirm the reset if any previous entries display in the dialog box.

Ⓑ **Click** in the Set Objective box (if not already selected), and select **cell B15** in the worksheet.

Ⓒ Choose **Value Of** and enter **650000** in the text box to set a specific total financed cost.

Ⓓ Click in the **By Changing Cells** box and select **cell B3** (the site plan cost) in the worksheet.

Ⓔ Type a **comma** and click in **cell B7** (the interest rate) in the worksheet.

Ⓕ Click the **Add** button to display the Add Constraint dialog box.

5. Follow these steps to specify a constraint:

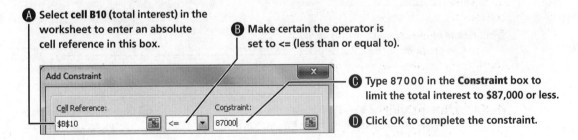

Ⓐ Select **cell B10** (total interest) in the worksheet to enter an absolute cell reference in this box.

Ⓑ Make certain the operator is set to <= (less than or equal to).

Ⓒ Type 87000 in the **Constraint** box to limit the total interest to $87,000 or less.

Ⓓ Click OK to complete the constraint.

6. Take a moment to review the options you have set in the Solver Parameters dialog box.

7. Click the **Solve** button, and the Solver will go to work.

8. Follow these steps to accept the proposed solution:

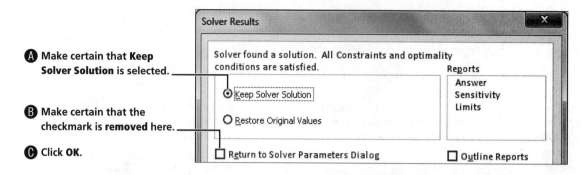

Ⓐ Make certain that **Keep Solver Solution** is selected.

Ⓑ Make certain that the checkmark is **removed** here.

Ⓒ Click **OK**.

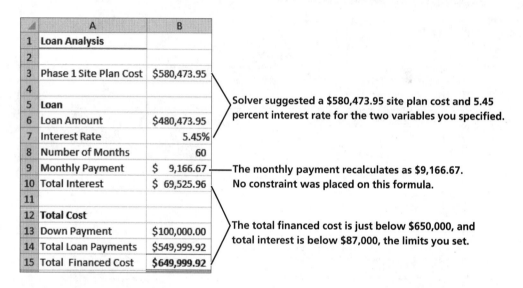

Solver suggested a $580,473.95 site plan cost and 5.45 percent interest rate for the two variables you specified.

The monthly payment recalculates as $9,166.67. No constraint was placed on this formula.

The total financed cost is just below $650,000, and total interest is below $87,000, the limits you set.

9. Choose **Data→Analysis→Solver** [?] from the Ribbon.

10. Click **Reset All** to clear the previous options, and click **OK** to confirm.

11. Follow these guidelines to set options in the Solver Parameters dialog box:

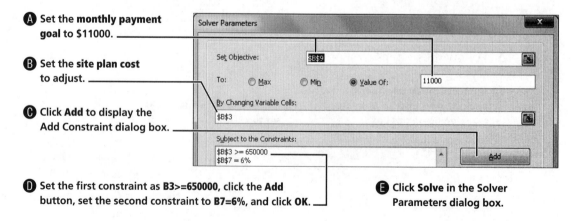

Ⓐ Set the **monthly payment goal** to $11000.

Ⓑ Set the **site plan cost** to adjust.

Ⓒ Click **Add** to display the Add Constraint dialog box.

Ⓓ Set the first constraint as **B3>=650000**, click the **Add** button, set the second constraint to **B7=6%**, and click **OK**.

Ⓔ Click **Solve** in the Solver Parameters dialog box.

12. Choose **Restore Original Values** make certain that the checkmark is removed next to Return to Solver Parameters Dialog, and click **OK**.

13. In **cell B7**, change the interest rate to **6%**.

14. Choose **Data→Analysis→Solver** ![solver icon].

15. If necessary, select the constraint rule **$B$7=6%**, and click the **Delete** button.

16. Click **Solve** to use the other options that you previously set.

17. Click **OK** to accept the proposed solution.

18. **Save** ![save icon] the changes to the workbook.

19. Take a few minutes to experiment with Solver.

20. When you have finished, **close** ![close icon] the workbook **without** saving changes.

Scenario Manager

Excel provides the Scenario Manager to create and save what-if models with up to 32 variables. This allows you to model virtually any what-if scenario. Scenario Manager does not solve for a specific variable value to achieve a formula result as Goal Seek and Solver do. You may, however, save a Solver solution as a scenario.

What Is a Scenario?

A scenario is a group of values assigned to cells in a what-if model. The model calculates formula results based on the values you enter in the scenario. Scenarios are given names to identify them, and they are saved and organized using the Scenario Manager.

Managing Scenarios

You may create and manage a large number of scenarios in the Scenario Manager. This way, you may compare various scenarios and the results they achieve. The Scenario Manager also lets you display and print a summary of all scenarios. The scenario summary does not automatically update when you change any scenario values. You must create a new summary.

Adding Scenarios

Selecting the variable cells in the worksheet before issuing the Scenario Manager command is recommended. The ⌐Ctrl key is used to select noncontiguous cell ranges. The Scenario Manager has an Add button that allows you to create new scenarios. Each scenario may contain different values. The following illustration shows the Scenario Values dialog box with values entered for the variable cells. If you enter a formula for a variable, Excel will convert the result to a value.

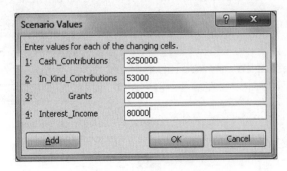

The entered values are applied to cells in the worksheet, thus forming a scenario.

Hands-On 2.4: Use the Scenario Manager

1. **Open** the Campaign Scenarios workbook from the Lesson 02 folder.

2. In the **Campaign Analysis** worksheet, enter the model values in the **range B4:B7** as shown.

	A	B
1	Capital Campaign Net Income Model	
2		
3	*Income Goals*	
4	Cash Contributions	1,000,000
5	In-Kind Contributions	50,000
6	Grants	30,000
7	Interest Income	20,000
8	Total Income	$ 1,100,000

3. Select **cell B17**, and review the formula =B8-B15 in the Formula Bar.

4. In **cell B18**, enter the formula **=B15/B8**.

5. Format **cell B18** as **bold** and **Percent Style** with **two decimal places**.

6. Select the **range A4:B8**, which includes the income labels and the cell values to which they refer.

7. With the **range A4:B8** still selected, **hold down** ⎡Ctrl⎤ and select the **range A17:B18**, which includes labels and formula cells.

	A	B
1	Capital Campaign Net Income Model	
2		
3	*Income Goals*	
4	Cash Contributions	1,000,000
5	In-Kind Contributions	50,000
6	Grants	30,000
7	Interest Income	20,000
8	Total Income	$ 1,100,000
9		
10	*Targeted Expenses*	
11	Web/Social Media Development	25,000
12	Print Materials	10,000
13	Events	50,000
14	Salaries - Grant Proposals	25,000
15	Total Expenses	$ 110,000
16		
17	Projected Net Income	$ 990,000
18	Targeted Expenses vs. Income	10.00%

8. Choose **Formulas→Defined Names→Create From Selection** ⊞ from the Ribbon.

9. Place a checkmark in the **Left Column box** (if not already checked) and click **OK**.

10. Choose **Formulas→Defined Names→Name Manager** 🖨 to view all defined names and their Refers To entries.

11. Widen the **Name** column and **Refers To** column, if necessary, to view entire entries in the Name Manager dialog box.

12. Close the **Name Manager** dialog box.

13. Taking care not to select cell B8, select the **range B4:B7** as shown to the right.

14. Choose **Data→Data Tools→What-If Analysis** 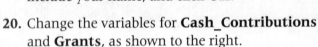 **→Scenario Manager** from the Ribbon.

	A	B
3	*Income Goals*	
4	**Cash Contributions**	1,000,000
5	**In-Kind Contributions**	50,000
6	**Grants**	30,000
7	**Interest Income**	20,000
8	Total Income	$ 1,100,000

15. Click the **Add** button to add a new scenario.

16. Follow these steps to set scenario options in the Add Scenario dialog box:

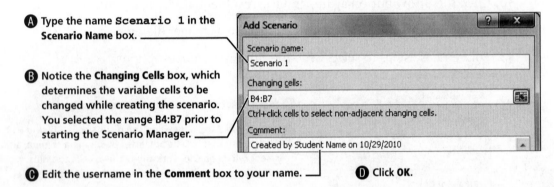

Ⓐ Type the name **Scenario 1** in the **Scenario Name** box.

Ⓑ Notice the **Changing Cells** box, which determines the variable cells to be changed while creating the scenario. You selected the range **B4:B7** prior to starting the Scenario Manager.

Ⓒ Edit the username in the **Comment** box to your name.

Ⓓ Click **OK**.

17. Click **OK** to complete the scenario.

18. Click the **Add** button in the Scenario Manager dialog box.

19. Enter the name **Scenario 2** in the **Add Scenario** dialog box, make certain the Changing Cells are **B4:B7**, edit the Comment to include your name, and click **OK**.

20. Change the variables for **Cash_Contributions** and **Grants**, as shown to the right.

21. Click **OK** in the Scenario Values box.

22. Make certain **Scenario 2** is chosen, and click the **Show** button in the Scenario Manager dialog box. (Move the dialog box to view the worksheet values, if necessary.)

23. Choose **Scenario 1** and click the **Show** button.

24. Now add **two new scenarios** using the data in the following table:

Variable	Scenario 3 Scenario Value	Scenario 4 Scenario Value
Cash Contributions	500,000	3,250,000
In-Kind Contributions	25,000	53,000
Grants	25,000	200,000
Interest Income	25,000	80,000

25. Use the **Show** button to display the results of each scenario.

26. Choose **Scenario 3** in the Scenario Manager dialog box and click the **Show** button.

27. With **Scenario 3** still chosen, click the **Edit** button.

28. Click **OK** in the Edit Scenario box.

29. Change the **Cash Contributions** value to **2000000** in the Scenario Values dialog box and click **OK**.

30. Click the **Show** button again, and the result equals 5.30 percent.

31. Click the **Summary** button in the Scenario Manager dialog box.

32. Follow these steps to select Scenario Summary report options:

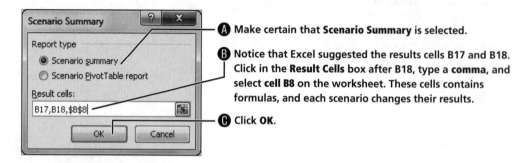

Ⓐ Make certain that **Scenario Summary** is selected.

Ⓑ Notice that Excel suggested the results cells B17 and B18. Click in the **Result Cells** box after B18, type a **comma**, and select **cell B8** on the worksheet. These cells contains formulas, and each scenario changes their results.

Ⓒ Click **OK**.

33. **Save** 🖫 and **close** the workbook.

Concepts Review

Concepts Review   labyrinthelab.com/fastcourse_excel10

To check your knowledge of the key concepts introduced in this lesson, complete the Concepts Review quiz by going to the URL listed above.

Notes

LESSON 3
Using Advanced Formatting and Analysis Tools

In this lesson, you will consolidate data from detail worksheets by position and category. Occasionally, you may need to set up multiple worksheets before data common to all of them are available. You will group worksheets to enter the data into them simultaneously. Excel's Data Validation tool can assist users of all levels with data entry by forcing values to fall within a specified range. When data are combined or imported from different sources, duplicate records may exist. Excel's Remove Duplicates tool can delete them. Data tables assist with what-if analyses by adjusting variables in a formula. Trendlines are another aid to analysis, helping you perceive and forecast trends in chart data. You also will create sparklines, or mini charts, to present changing data patterns in cells right next to the worksheet data.

LESSON TIMING

- Concepts/Hands-On: 1 hr 30 min
- Concepts Review: 15 min
- Total: 1 hr 45 min

LEARNING OBJECTIVES

After studying this lesson, you will be able to:

- Group worksheets for efficient data entry
- Consolidate data from multiple worksheets by position and category
- Set data validation rules to restrict data entry
- Remove duplicate records from data
- Create data tables to perform what-if analyses
- Develop trendlines and sparklines to analyze chart data

CASE STUDY: CONSOLIDATING AND VALIDATING DATA

Sandra Chavez-Hall will present quarterly fundraising results to Raritan Clinic East's foundation board using charts and tables. Sandra needs a workbook to store detailed contribution information in separate sheets. She will use consolidation features to automatically summarize the data into a summary sheet. She will use data validation and other tools to format the workbook and create sparklines and will use a data table to forecast net income for an upcoming fundraising event.

Working with Grouped Worksheets

You may temporarily group two or more worksheets to save time when entering data, creating formulas, and formatting worksheets. When worksheets are grouped, whatever you type is entered on all sheets simultaneously. The same is true of formatting. For example, changing the column width on one worksheet also affects the same column on the other grouped worksheets. You may copy data from an ungrouped worksheet and paste to all worksheets in a group.

Grouping Worksheets

By grouping worksheets, you work with them as a set. For example, imagine that you used a budget template to create a workbook with 12 monthly worksheets. Rather than typing or pasting the same row labels multiple times, you may group the sheets and type the labels just once. You may group contiguous or noncontiguous worksheets using the [Shift] and [Ctrl] keys, just as you do when selecting multiple cells. In this lesson, you will work with contiguous worksheets. When worksheets are grouped, their sheet tabs change color, and *[Group]* displays in the window's title bar.

	A	B	C	D
4	**Pledge Level**	**Q1**	**Q2**	
5	Level 1	5,176,926	5,026,177	9,93
6	Level 2	-	-	1,00
7	Level 3	100,000	100,000	2

The title bar indicates that worksheets are grouped.

The sheet tabs turn white when worksheets are grouped.

Ungrouping Worksheets

Grouping and ungrouping actually are selecting and deselecting procedures. The Ungroup Sheets command in the sheet tab pop-up, or context, menu removes the grouping so that you may work in one worksheet at a time.

 ## Hands-On 3.1: Group Worksheets

1. **Start** Excel and **open** the Quarterly Summary workbook from the Lesson 03 folder in your file storage location.

2. Take a few moments to study the **Summary** and **three source** worksheets.

3. Follow these steps to group the four worksheets:

Ⓐ Click the **Summary** sheet tab.

| Summary / Cash / In-Kind / Grants —Ⓑ **Hold down** [Shift] **and click the Grants sheet tab. Release** [Shift].

4. In **cell A14**, type `Web/Social Media Development` and **tap** [Enter].

5. Continue entering the following labels in **cells A15:A17**: `Print Materials`, `Events`, and `Salaries - Grant Proposals`.

6. In **cell B4**, type **Q1** and **right-align** the label. Apply **bold**.

7. Use **AutoFill** to extend the series through **cell E4**.

8. **Deselect** the highlighted cells.

9. **Right-click** the Summary sheet tab and choose **Ungroup Sheets** from the context menu.

10. Display each of the **source** worksheets.

11. Display the **Summary** worksheet.

12. Select the **range A5:A10**, and use Ctrl+C to copy.

13. Display the **Cash** worksheet and select **cell A5**, the destination cell.

14. **Hold down** Shift and click the **Grants** sheet tab to select all source sheets.

15. Use Ctrl+V to paste.

16. Deselect the cells.

17. Display the **Summary** worksheet.

18. **Tap** Esc to clear the marquee surrounding the **range A5:A10**.

19. **Group** the four worksheets again.

20. Follow these steps to select the desired cells to format:

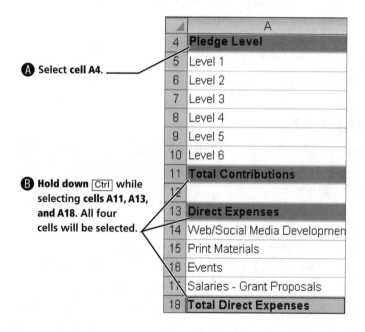

A Select cell A4.

B Hold down Ctrl while selecting **cells A11, A13, and A18**. All four cells will be selected.

21. Choose **Home→Styles→Cell Styles→Themed Cell Styles→20% - Accent6**, and then apply **Bold** from the Ribbon.

22. **Deselect** the cells.

23. Take a few moments to view the changes that were made to each worksheet.

24. Experiment with **grouping** and **ungrouping** contiguous and noncontiguous sheets.

25. When finished, make certain to **ungroup** the worksheets.

26. Save 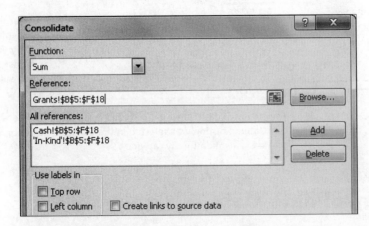 the changes, and leave the workbook **open**.

Consolidating Worksheet Data

Excel's Consolidate command combines values from source worksheets into a destination worksheet. You select an entire range, and all its value and formula cells (but not text cells) are consolidated simultaneously to the destination worksheet. Only one range may be consolidated from each source worksheet. The calculation results are values rather than formulas unless you select the Create Links to Source Data option. When the results are values, you must repeat the Consolidate command if values change later in the source worksheets. You may redisplay the Consolidate dialog box to add a reference range for any worksheet added to the workbook, and you may delete any reference range.

A consolidation reference being created to the Grants worksheet in the Consolidate dialog box

Consolidation Functions

The SUM function is the most commonly used consolidation function. You also may use AVERAGE, MIN, MAX, and some other statistical functions when consolidating. You choose the desired function in the Consolidate dialog box when you set up the consolidation.

Types of Consolidation

You may consolidate data using either of the following methods:

- **By Position**—This method is useful when all worksheets have the same layout. To consolidate by position, specify the same range in all worksheets. Excel uses the function you choose to consolidate values in the same cell of each of the specified worksheets.

- **By Category**—This method is used when the supporting worksheets have different layouts but identical row or column labels that refer to the common data. A worksheet may contain labels for categories that other worksheets do not include. Excel uses the row and column headings to determine which rows or columns to consolidate with the other consolidation ranges you specify. The consolidation produces one row or column in the summary sheet for each unique row or column encountered in the supporting sheets. The consolidated data contains no blank rows or text formatting from the source worksheets, but you can format the summary sheet results after the consolidation.

Creating Links to Source Data

By default, consolidated data is not linked to the source cells. The Create Links to Source Data option does create linking formulas on the summary worksheet. For example, cell C5 contains the linking formula =Cash!$B$5 as shown in the following illustration. The consolidated data are formatted as an outline that may be expanded to view the source data or collapsed to view the totals. Any changes to source data on the original worksheets will update in the summary sheet.

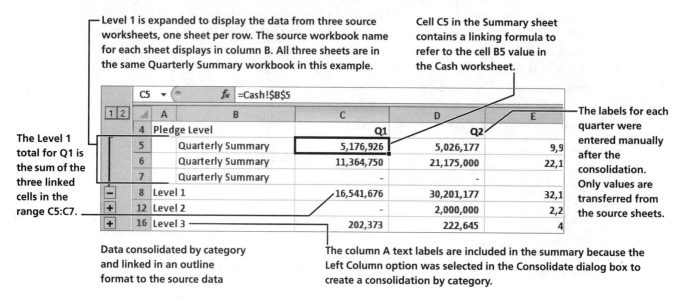

Level 1 is expanded to display the data from three source worksheets, one sheet per row. The source workbook name for each sheet displays in column B. All three sheets are in the same Quarterly Summary workbook in this example.

Cell C5 in the Summary sheet contains a linking formula to refer to the cell B5 value in the Cash worksheet.

The Level 1 total for Q1 is the sum of the three linked cells in the range C5:C7.

The labels for each quarter were entered manually after the consolidation. Only values are transferred from the source sheets.

Data consolidated by category and linked in an outline format to the source data

The column A text labels are included in the summary because the Left Column option was selected in the Consolidate dialog box to create a consolidation by category.

Hands-On 3.2: Consolidate Data

1. Display the **Summary** worksheet in the Quarterly Summary workbook.

2. Select **cell B5** as the starting point for the consolidated data.

3. Choose **Data→Data Tools→Consolidate** from the Ribbon.

4. If necessary, move the **Consolidate** dialog box until **cell B5** in the Summary sheet and the sheet tabs at the bottom of the Excel window are visible.

5. Follow these steps to set consolidation options in the Consolidate dialog box:

Ⓐ Drop down the **Function** menu, review the choices, and make certain that **Sum** is selected.

Ⓑ Click in the **Reference** box.

Ⓒ Click the **Cash** sheet tab and select the **range B5:F18**.

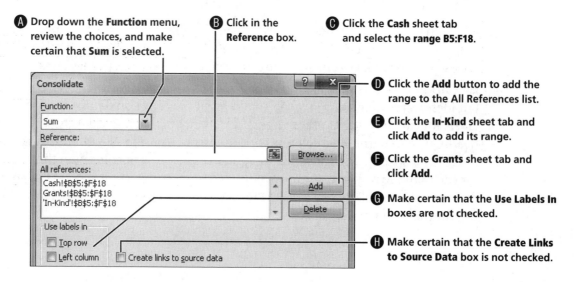

Ⓓ Click the **Add** button to add the range to the All References list.

Ⓔ Click the **In-Kind** sheet tab and click **Add** to add its range.

Ⓕ Click the **Grants** sheet tab and click **Add**.

Ⓖ Make certain that the **Use Labels In** boxes are not checked.

Ⓗ Make certain that the **Create Links to Source Data** box is not checked.

6. Click **OK**.

	Pledge Level	Q1	Q2	Q3	Q4	
4	Pledge Level	Q1	Q2	Q3	Q4	
5	Level 1	16,541,676	30,201,177	32,114,970	38,409,659	
6	Level 2	–	2,000,000	2,253,988	2,000,075	
7	Level 3	202,373	222,645	479,673	412,892	
8	Level 4	100,891	50,000	51,209	–	
9	Level 5	8,647	13,043	17,921	18,676	
10	Level 6	1,262	2,889	4,600	6,435	
11	Total Contributions	16,854,849	32,489,754	34,922,361	40,847,737	125,114,701
12						
13	Direct Expenses					
14	Web/Social Media Developmen	3,500	3,500	3,500	37,000	
15	Print Materials	947	977	1,699	864	
16	Events	12,589	22,753	10,465	45,872	
17	Salaries - Grant Proposals	6,000	6,000	6,000	6,000	
18	Total Direct Expenses	23,036	33,230	21,664	89,736	167,666

7. Select any cell in the **range B5:F18** in the Summary worksheet.

8. Save 💾 the changes, and leave the workbook **open**.

Working with Data Validation

Excel's data validation tool lets you restrict data entry in cells. The default validation setting for a cell is Any Value, meaning that until you specify a validation setting and criteria, any value may be entered in the cell.

Restricting Data Entry Using Criteria

You may restrict both the type and range of acceptable values. For example, you may want to restrict data entry to whole numbers between 0 and 100,000. You may also create an input message and error alert message to guide the user in entering acceptable data. An input message appears whenever the restricted cell is selected. An error message appears whenever data entry is attempted and the data is not of the correct type or within the accepted range.

The following table describes the available validation criteria.

Type	Entries Must Be
Any Value	No restrictions; may display an input message without checking for valid entries
Custom	A formula, expression, or reference to a calculation in another cell
Dates	Dates
Decimal	Numbers or fractions
List	Only those in a specified list
Text Length	A specific number of characters
Time	Times
Whole Number	Integers without decimal places

Copying a Data Validation Rule

A data validation rule must be created while a single worksheet is selected and cannot be set up while worksheets are grouped. You may, however, copy a cell containing a validation rule. Then, you may use the Validation option of the Paste Special command on the Ribbon to apply a data validation rule from that cell to other cells on the same worksheet, another sheet, or grouped sheets. You may edit a validation rule. The Apply These Changes to All Other Cells with the Same Settings option in the Data Validation dialog box updates cells only in the active worksheet. You must use the Validation option of the Paste Special command to apply the revised rule to cells on other sheets.

Hands-On 3.3: Set Up Data Validation

1. Display the **Cash** worksheet of the Quarterly Summary workbook.

2. Select the values in the **range B14:E17** as shown in the following illustration. (Make certain that the expense labels in column A and the total cells in row 18 are **not** selected.)

⊿	A	B	C	D	E
14	Web/Social Media Development	1,500	1,500	1,500	35,000
15	Print Materials	500	500	500	563
16	Events	12,321	22,753	10,465	45,657
17	Salaries - Grant Proposals	-	-	-	-
18	**Total Direct Expenses**	**14,321**	**24,753**	**12,465**	**81,220**

3. Choose **Data→Data Tools→Data Validation** 📋 from the Ribbon.

4. Follow these steps to set the data entry restrictions:

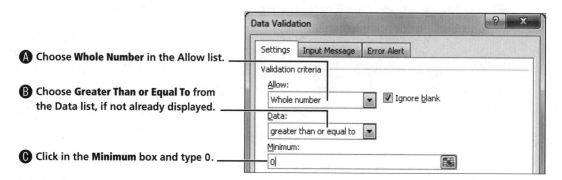

Ⓐ Choose **Whole Number** in the Allow list.

Ⓑ Choose **Greater Than or Equal To** from the Data list, if not already displayed.

Ⓒ Click in the **Minimum** box and type 0.

5. Display the **Input Message** tab in the dialog box.

6. Display the **Error Alert** tab.

7. Follow these steps to set an error alert message:

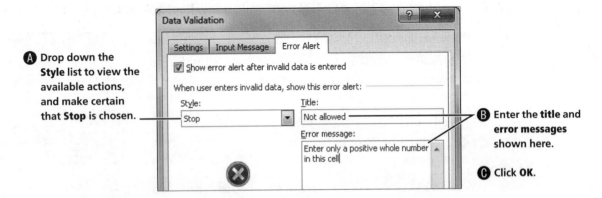

A Drop down the **Style** list to view the available actions, and make certain that **Stop** is chosen.

B Enter the **title** and error messages shown here.

C Click **OK**.

8. Select **cell B14** in the **Cash** sheet.

9. Type the negative number **−1000** and **tap** ⎡Enter⎤.

10. Click the **Retry** button in the message box.

11. Type **1000.50** and **tap** ⎡Enter⎤.

12. Click the **Retry** button and **enter** the original number **1500**.

13. Select the **range A5:A10**.

14. Choose **Data→Data Tools→Data Validation** from the Ribbon.

15. Follow these steps to set up the data entry restriction:

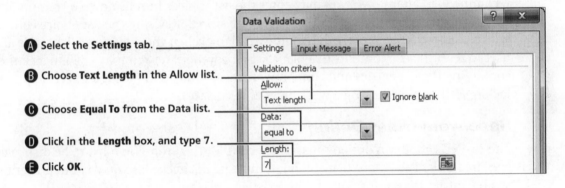

A Select the **Settings** tab.

B Choose **Text Length** in the Allow list.

C Choose **Equal To** from the Data list.

D Click in the **Length** box, and type 7.

E Click **OK**.

16. Select **cell A5**.

17. Type **Level 22** and **tap** ⎡Enter⎤.

18. Click the **Cancel** button in the error message dialog box to leave the original entry unchanged.

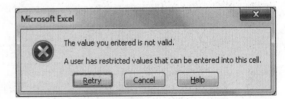

19. Right-click cell B14, and choose **Copy** from the context menu.

20. Select the **In-Kind** sheet tab, **hold down** ⎡Shift⎤, and select the **Grants** sheet tab.

21. Select the **range B14:E17**.

22. Choose **Home→Clipboard→Paste menu ▾→Paste Special** from the Ribbon.

23. Choose **Validation** in the Paste Special dialog box, and click **OK**.

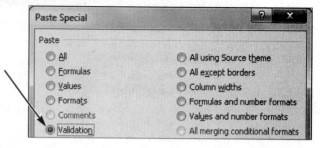

24. Select **cell B14** to deselect the range in both grouped sheets.

25. **Right-click** the Grants sheet tab, and choose **Ungroup Sheets** from the context menu.

26. Type **web** in cell B14 of the **Grants** worksheet, and **tap** Enter.

27. Click **Cancel** in the error message dialog box to restore the original value.

28. Save 💾 the changes, and leave the workbook **open**.

Creating Drop-Down Lists for Data Entry

The data validation List option allows you to restrict data entry for a cell to a choice contained in a drop-down list. For example, the acceptable entries for a product's status could be *In Stock* and *Reorder*. An error message displays if the user attempts to type an entry.

Specifying List Items

You may type the list items separated by commas (,) in the Data Validation dialog box. As a recommended alternative, you may enter the list choices in cells down a column of a worksheet and give the range where the entries are stored. Revising the list choices often is easier with the in-worksheet method. Including a blank cell at the end of the list range allows the user to reset the cell contents to a blank when appropriate. You may wish to lock the cell range containing the list entries and turn on worksheet protection (see the Excel Help topic about locking cells and protecting a worksheet, if necessary).

Specifying Other Options

The In-Cell Dropdown option must be checked for the drop-down list to be displayed in the specified cells. The Ignore Blanks option must be unchecked if you wish to prevent users from typing entries in cells formatted with a list.

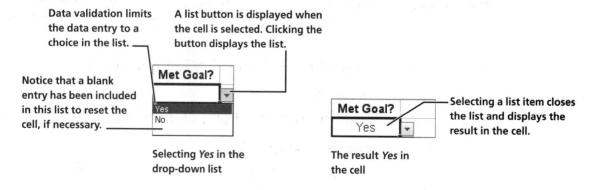

Data validation limits the data entry to a choice in the list.

A list button is displayed when the cell is selected. Clicking the button displays the list.

Notice that a blank entry has been included in this list to reset the cell, if necessary.

Selecting *Yes* in the drop-down list

Selecting a list item closes the list and displays the result in the cell.

The result *Yes* in the cell

Hands-On 3.4: Use a Drop-Down List

1. Display the **Summary** worksheet of the Quarterly Summary workbook.

2. Type **Yes** in **cell G1**.

3. Type **No** in **cell G2**.

4. Select the **range G1:G3**.

5. Click in the **Name** box to the left of the Formula Bar.

6. Type **List** and **tap** [Enter] to assign the name to the range.

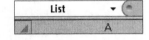

7. In **cell G4**, type **Met Goal?** Center align the entry, and choose **bold**, if necessary.

8. Select the **range G5:G10**; **center-align** the cells.

9. Choose **Data→Data Tools→Data Validation** ⊞ from the Ribbon.

10. Follow these steps to set up the data entry restriction:

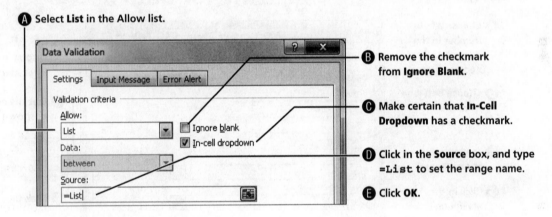

Ⓐ Select **List** in the Allow list.

Ⓑ Remove the checkmark from **Ignore Blank**.

Ⓒ Make certain that **In-Cell Dropdown** has a checkmark.

Ⓓ Click in the **Source** box, and type **=List** to set the range name.

Ⓔ Click **OK**.

11. Select **cell G5**.

12. Follow these steps to enter data from the drop-down list:

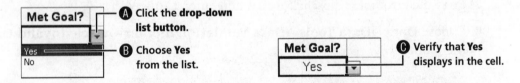

Ⓐ Click the **drop-down list button**.

Ⓑ Choose **Yes** from the list.

Ⓒ Verify that **Yes** displays in the cell.

13. Select **cell G6**, and choose **No** from the in-cell drop-down list.

14. Select **cell G7**, and choose **No**.

15. Click the **drop-down list button** on **cell G7**, and choose the **blank item** below No.

16. Select **cell G8**, type **Maybe**, and **tap** [Enter].

17. Read the error message, and click **Cancel**.

18. **Save** 🖫 the changes, and leave the workbook **open**.

Circling Invalid Data

At times, data may already be entered in worksheet cells before data validation rules are created. Some cells then may contain invalid data, so you should use the Circle Invalid Data command to find them. The command does just what the name implies: it places circles around any data that does not conform to the validation rules set for the cells. Once the data is circled, you may ignore or correct an entry. The red circles are easy to spot and do not print.

Hands-On 3.5: Circle Invalid Data

1. Display the **Cash** worksheet of the Quarterly Summary workbook.

2. Taking care not to select the totals in row 18, select the expense values in the **range B14:E17**.

3. Choose **Data→Data Tools→Data Validation** 📷 from the Ribbon.

4. Display the **Settings** tab in the Data Validation dialog box, if necessary.

5. Follow these steps to restrict expense values to a maximum of $32,000:

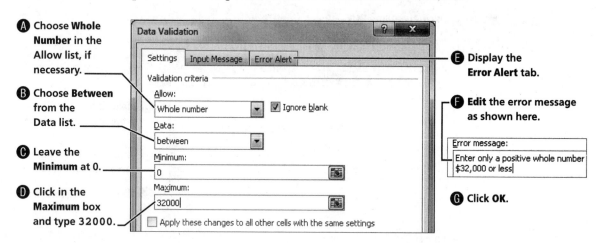

6. Enter **41500** in **cell B15**.

7. Read the error message, click **Retry**, and enter **1200**.

8. Choose **Data→Data Tools→Data Validation menu ▾→Circle Invalid Data** 🔢 from the Ribbon.

13	Direct Expenses				
14	Web/Social Media Development	1,500	1,500	1,500	35,000
15	Print Materials	1,200	500	500	563
16	Events	12,321	22,753	10,465	45,657
17	Salaries - Grant Proposals	-	-	-	-

9. Select **cell E14** and enter **1500**.

10. Leave the value in **cell E16** as is.

11. Choose **Data→Data Tools→Data Validation menu ▾→Clear Validation Circles** from the Ribbon.

12. Display the **Summary** worksheet.

13. Select **cell B5**.

14. Choose **Data→Data Tools→Consolidate** from the Ribbon.

15. Click **OK**.

16. **Save** the changes, and **close** the workbook.

Removing Duplicate Records

When you combine or import records into a worksheet, duplicate records may then exist in multiple rows of the worksheet. Excel provides several methods to identify and remove duplicates that contain the same cell entries as those in another row. The records are not considered duplicates if the data are formatted differently.

Filtering for Unique Records

You may perform an advanced filter to temporarily hide duplicate records. You may filter a list or table in place, as shown in the following illustration. You also may choose to copy unique records to another area of the same worksheet or a different worksheet.

Duplicate records in rows 5 and 7 are hidden temporarily.

	A	B	C
3	Pledge Level	Team Leader	Sponsor Category
4	Level 5	Abbott	Organization Contrib
6	Level 4	Faber	Corporate Sponsors
8	Level 1	Lemus	Federal Government
9	Level 3	Faber	Corporate Sponsors
10	Level 6	Nguyen	Individual Contributio

The result of an advanced filter for unique records

Removing Duplicates

The Remove Duplicates command on the Ribbon deletes duplicate records from a list. You specify the columns in which Excel is to look for an exact match. Choosing all columns will ensure that only the records that match in every cell will be deleted. You may undo the action if the result is not what you expect.

 ## Hands-On 3.6: Filter Records and Remove Duplicates

1. **Open** the Combined Contributions workbook from the Lesson 03 folder.

2. Select **cell D4**.

3. Choose **Data→Sort & Filter→Advanced** from the Ribbon.

4. Follow these steps to filter the list for unique records:

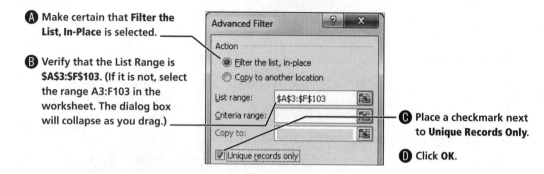

Ⓐ Make certain that **Filter the List, In-Place** is selected.

Ⓑ Verify that the List Range is **$A$3:$F$103**. (If it is not, select the range A3:F103 in the worksheet. The dialog box will collapse as you drag.)

Ⓒ Place a checkmark next to **Unique Records Only**.

Ⓓ Click **OK**.

	A	B	C
3	**Pledge Level**	**Team Leader**	**Sponsor Category**
4	Level 5	Abbott	Organization Contrib
6	Level 4	Faber	Corporate Sponsors
8	Level 1	Lemus	Federal Government
9	Level 3	Faber	Corporate Sponsors
10	Level 6	Nguyen	Individual Contributio

Sponsors Table
Ready   98 of 100 records found

5. Choose **Data→Sort & Filter→Clear** 🧹 from the Ribbon.

6. Make certain that **cell D4** or another cell in the list is selected.

7. Choose **Data→Data Tools→Remove Duplicates** from the Ribbon.

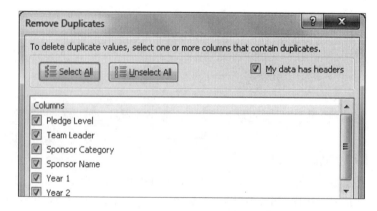

Remove Duplicates

To delete duplicate values, select one or more columns that contain duplicates.

[Select All] [Unselect All]   ☑ My data has headers

Columns
☑ Pledge Level
☑ Team Leader
☑ Sponsor Category
☑ Sponsor Name
☑ Year 1
☑ Year 2

8. Make certain **My Data Has Headers** has a checkmark in the upper-right corner of the dialog box, and click **OK**.

9. Read the message indicating that two records were removed, and click **OK**.

10. Save 💾 and **close** the workbook.

Using Data Tables

Data tables are different from the tables that allow you to sort, filter, and create totals for data. Data tables preview the effect that changing some values would have on a formula's result. A data table is structured around a specific formula to perform a what-if analysis. Various values from a list are substituted for either one or two cell references in the formula. The Data Table command calculates the formula result for each value listed.

One-Variable Data Tables

One-variable data tables compute results for various values substituted for a cell reference in a formula. For example, the data table may display the result for a FV (Future Value) formula with the monthly payment as a variable in increments of $20. This example is shown in the following illustration, where the empty Payment cell (B5) is known as the input cell. Each value from Payment column C of the data table is substituted in the input cell, and its corresponding Future Value result displays in column D.

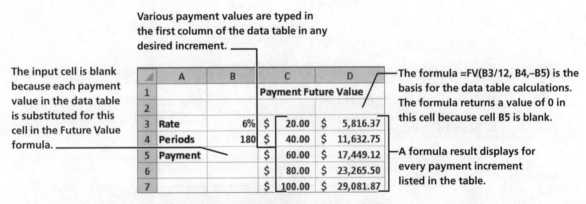

A one-variable data table for a Future Value formula

Two-Variable Data Tables

You will work with two-variable data tables in this lesson. While a one-variable data table has one input cell, this type has two input cells. Values are substituted for two cell references in the formula. The following illustration shows the layout of a two-variable data table using the same Future Value formula as in the previous example. Take a few moments to review this illustration carefully.

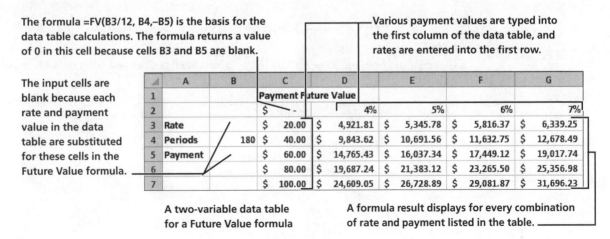

A two-variable data table for a Future Value formula

A formula result displays for every combination of rate and payment listed in the table.

Hands-On 3.7: Create a Two-Variable Data Table

1. **Open** a new, blank workbook.

2. Enter the following data into **Sheet1**, formatting the numbers and text as shown.

	A	B	C	D	E	F	G
1	Net Income $ Goal	Net Income % Goal					
2	$ 75,000	70%					
3				Ticket Sales Above (Below) Goal			
4			Tickets Sold				
5			600	650	700	750	800
6	Ticket Price	$ 100					
7		$ 150					
8		$ 200					
9		$ 250					
10		$ 300					

3. Select **cell B5**.

4. **Enter** the formula **=(B2*B3*B4)-A2** in **cell B5**.

5. Select **cell B5**, and change the text color to **white** to **hide** the formula result.

6. Select the **range B5:G10** as shown.

	A	B	C	D	E	F	G
4			Tickets Sold				
5			600	650	700	750	800
6	Ticket Price	$ 100					
7		$ 150					
8		$ 200					
9		$ 250					
10		$ 300					

7. Choose **Data→Data Tools→What-If Analysis →Data Table** from the Ribbon.

8. Follow these steps to choose the input cells:

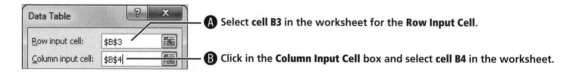

Data Table

Row input cell: $B$3 — **A** Select **cell B3** in the worksheet for the **Row Input Cell**.

Column input cell: $B$4 — **B** Click in the **Column Input Cell** box and select **cell B4** in the worksheet.

9. Click **OK** in the Data Table dialog box.

	A	B	C	D	E	F	G
3				Ticket Sales Above (Below) Goal			
4			Tickets Sold				
5			600	650	700	750	800
6	Ticket Price	$ 100	(33,000)	(29,500)	(26,000)	(22,500)	(19,000)
7		$ 150	(12,000)	(6,750)	(1,500)	3,750	9,000
8		$ 200	9,000	16,000	23,000	30,000	37,000
9		$ 250	30,000	38,750	47,500	56,250	65,000
10		$ 300	51,000	61,500	72,000	82,500	93,000

10. Select the **range C6:G10**, and choose **Comma Style with no decimals** from the Ribbon.

11. **Save** the changes as `Tickets Data Table` in the Lesson 03 folder in your file storage location.

12. Feel free to experiment with your data table. For example, try changing the ticket prices in **column B** to increments of $25 rather than $50. How would the results change if the net income percentage in cell B2 were 65%?

13. When you are finished, **close** the workbook **without** saving again.

Creating Trendlines

Trendlines are used on charts for data analysis and prediction. A trendline visually displays the trend (increasing or decreasing) of one data series in a chart. There are several types of trendlines available, each suited to the display of particular types of data. For example, a linear trendline works well with data that follow a fairly straight path. A moving average trendline smoothes out fluctuations in data by averaging two or more adjacent data points for each trendline data point.

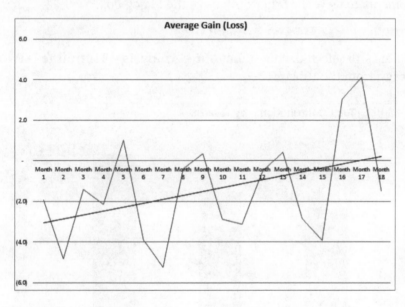

This linear trendline depicts the upward trend for average weight of patients enrolled in a clinical study over 18 months.

Hands-On 3.8: Add a Trendline

1. **Open** the Contributions Trend workbook from the Lesson 03 folder.

2. Display the **Trend Chart** worksheet.

3. **Select** the chart.

4. Choose **Chart Tools Layout→Analysis→Trendline** ▨ **→Linear Trendline** from the Ribbon.

5. Taking care to position the tip of the pointer arrow against the trendline as shown, select the **trendline**. (If the trendline does not display handles at its endpoints, reposition the tip of the mouse pointer at the trendline and select again.)

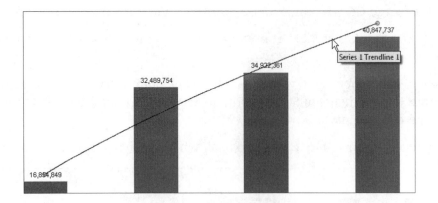

6. Choose **Layout→Analysis→Trendline→Linear Forecast Trendline**.

7. Select the trendline, and choose **Layout→Analysis→Trendline 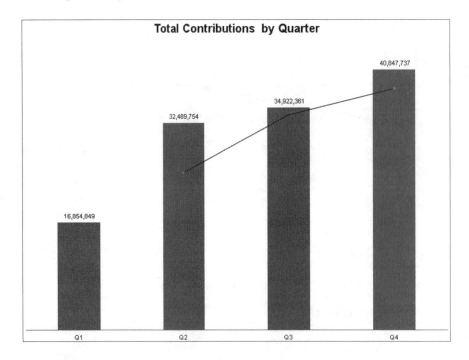→More Trendline Options** from the Ribbon.

8. In the **Forecast** area in the lower part of the Format Trendline dialog box, change **Forward** from 2.0 periods to **1**.

9. Take a few moments to view the other options in the dialog box.

10. Click **Close**.

11. With the trendline still selected, choose **Layout→Analysis→Trendline→Two Period Moving Average** from the Ribbon.

Total Contributions by Quarter

			40,847,737
		34,922,361	
	32,489,754		
16,854,849			
Q1	Q2	Q3	Q4

12. **Save** 💾 the changes, and leave the workbook **open**.

Creating Sparklines in Cells

Sparklines appear as miniature charts in worksheet cells. New in Excel 2010, sparklines allow you to show the data graphically without all the steps required in creating a normal chart. You also may select a cell range and create sparklines for every row or column at once. Changes to data are reflected immediately in sparklines right next to the data. Each sparkline charts the data in one row or column.

	A	B	C	D	E	F
4	**Pledge Level**	**Q1**	**Q2**	**Q3**	**Q4**	**By Quarter**
5	Level 1	16,541,676	30,201,177	32,114,970	38,409,659	
6	Level 2	-	2,000,000	2,253,988	2,000,075	
7	Level 3	202,373	222,645	479,673	412,892	
8	Level 4	100,891	50,000	51,209	-	
9	Level 5	8,647	13,043	17,921	18,676	
10	Level 6	1,262	2,889	4,600	6,435	
11	**Total Contributions**	**16,854,849**	**32,489,754**	**34,922,361**	**40,847,737**	**125,114,701**

Sparklines in column F with dot markers to show upward and downward trends for each pledge level of contributions during the year

Formatting Sparklines

You may format sparklines as lines, columns, or win-loss columns. The win-loss format shows the increase or decrease as compared to a previous period. You may format sparklines with styles and choose to display data points in various ways. For example, the Markers option displays a dot for each value along a sparkline formatted as a line. The same formatting must be applied to sparklines created all at once, while unique formatting may be applied to each sparkline created one at a time.

Hands-On 3.9: Create Sparklines

1. Display the **Summary** sheet in the Contributions Trend workbook.

2. Select the **range F5:F10**.

3. Choose **Insert→Sparklines→Line** 📈 from the Ribbon.

4. Follow these steps to complete the Create Sparklines dialog box:

Ⓐ Move the dialog box, if necessary, to view **column B** in the worksheet.

Ⓑ For the Data Range, select the **range B5:E10** in the worksheet. (The dialog box will collapse as you drag.)

Ⓒ Make certain that the **Location Range is $F$5:$F$10**.

Ⓓ Click **OK**.

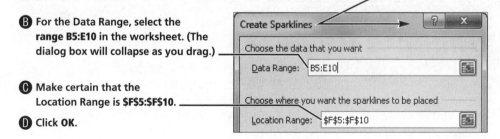

5. Choose **Sparkline Tools Design→Show→Markers** from the Ribbon to place a checkmark next to Markers.

6. Read the other options in the Design ribbon, and then **deselect** the range.

7. **Save** 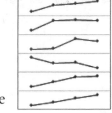 the changes.

8. Select **cell F14**, and choose **Insert→Sparklines→Column** 📊 from the Ribbon.

9. In the **Create Sparklines** dialog box, set the Data Range to **B14:E14**, verify that the Location Range is **$F$14**, and click **OK**.

10. Repeat **steps 8–9** to create a column sparkline in **cell F15**. Then, repeat twice more for **cells F16 and F17**.

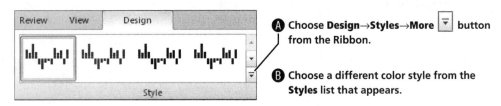

	B	C	D	E	F
13	Q1	Q2	Q3	Q4	By Quarter
14	3,500	3,500	3,500	37,000	
15	947	977	1,899	864	
16	12,589	22,753	10,465	45,872	
17	6,000	6,000	6,000	6,000	

11. Select **cell F15**, and follow these steps to change the sparkline style:

Ⓐ Choose **Design→Styles→More** button from the Ribbon.

Ⓑ Choose a different color style from the **Styles** list that appears.

12. Repeat the above step **twice** to apply different sparkline styles to **cells F16 and F17**.

13. Select **cell F5**.

14. Choose **Design→Style→More** button, and choose a different style from the Ribbon.

15. Feel free to experiment with any other options in the Show group of the Design ribbon to format the sparklines.

16. **Save** 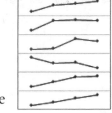 the changes, and **close** the workbook.

Concepts Review

Concepts Review   labyrinthelab.com/fastcourse_excel10

To check your knowledge of the key concepts introduced in this lesson, complete the Concepts Review quiz by going to the URL listed above.

Notes

LESSON 4
Collaborating in Excel

Collaboration is a common business activity. In this lesson, you will participate in workbook collaboration. You will set up folders for project files, place comments into an Excel workbook, and prepare the workbook for distribution. The ability to create shared workbooks is one of Excel's most powerful collaboration features. You can set up a workbook that several other users can access simultaneously on a network server, or intranet. Excel's change history tracking feature can help you avoid and resolve potential conflicts when data is edited by multiple users.

LEARNING OBJECTIVES

After studying this lesson, you will be able to:

- Create folders to organize project documents
- Manage and print comments in workbooks
- Track and consolidate changes made by multiple authors to a single workbook copy
- Prepare and share workbooks for collaboration
- Merge multiple versions of a shared workbook

LESSON TIMING

- Concepts/Hands-On: 1 hr 30 min
- Concepts Review: 15 min
- Total: 1 hr 45 min

CASE STUDY: COLLABORATING ON GRANT REPORTS

Grace Vargas is the grant and contract coordinator for Raritan Clinic East. She administers a Connections medical research grant project that involves Raritan's cardiology and orthopedics departments. She assembles financial data from both departments each quarter. Grace and her colleagues use email and an intranet to transmit information. They also use comments to ask questions and make suggestions. Grace may also share her workbook. As colleagues return revisions to the workbook, Grace uses Excel's Compare and Merge Workbooks command.

Creating Folders in Excel

When you work on a project, you usually will create one or more folders on your computer to store the documents and other types of files with which you will work. This topic will give you practice in creating folders and teach you techniques to access the new folders quickly.

Working with Project Folders

Depending on the size of the project and the number of files you must organize, you may need to create more than one folder. You may create a main folder for the project as well as subfolders inside of it for major types of documents or major sections of the project. The following diagram displays an example of project folders.

The Grant Project main folder for the project is selected in the address bar of the window. The folder contents appear below. ——

Subfolders hold documents for each quarterly report. ——

Various files that apply to the entire grant project are kept in the main folder ——

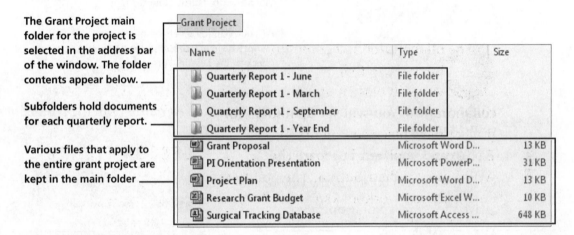

Creating Folders

You don't need to leave Excel to create a new folder. Simply choose the Open or Save As command, and then click the New Folder button (or Create New Folder button, depending on your Windows version) on the dialog box toolbar. You may create a single folder or several. If desired, you may also create folders inside other folders.

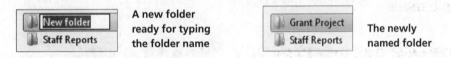

A new folder ready for typing the folder name

The newly named folder

Renaming Folders

You may rename folders from within Excel by right-clicking the folder and choosing Rename from the context menu. Or you may click once on the folder, pause one second, and click again to select the folder name for renaming.

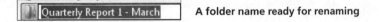
A folder name ready for renaming

Hands-On 4.1: Create and Rename a Project Folder

1. Start **Excel** and choose **File→Open** ⬚.

2. Follow these steps to begin creating the new folder:

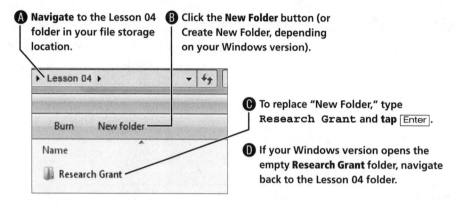

A **Navigate** to the Lesson 04 folder in your file storage location.

B Click the **New Folder** button (or Create New Folder, depending on your Windows version).

C To replace "New Folder," type **Research Grant** and **tap** Enter.

D If your Windows version opens the empty **Research Grant** folder, navigate back to the Lesson 04 folder.

3. **Right-click** the Research Grant folder and choose **Rename** from the bottom of the context menu.

4. Type **Grant Project** and **tap** Enter.

5. Click the **Cancel** button in the Open dialog box.

6. Leave the Excel window **open**.

Organizing Workbooks in Folders

Many computer users store their files in the Documents or My Documents folder found on most Windows systems. Sometimes you will store files in a separate folder such as the one you just created. This allows you to place your project on a portable drive to use at another computer. Excel's Open and Save As dialog boxes allow you to move or copy files to different folders and to delete files from within Excel.

Hands-On 4.2: Move and Copy Files to a Folder

1. Choose **File→Open** ⬚, and navigate to the Lesson 04 folder in your file storage location.

2. **Single-click** the Shared Budget file to select it.

3. Use Ctrl+X from the keyboard to cut the file.

4. **Double-click** the Grant Project folder to open it.

5. Use Ctrl+V from the keyboard to paste the file.

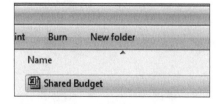

6. Navigate back to the Lesson 04 folder in the **Open** dialog box.

7. Follow these steps to copy the files:

A Scroll down the list, if necessary, until the **budget** files are visible.

B Select the **Connections Grant Cardiology Budget file.**

⊠	as-Animal Shelter Expenses
⊠	as-Crisis Intervention Budget
⊠	Connections Grant Cardiology Budget
⊠	ct-Bed Count
⊠	ct-Shared Bed Count Cardiology
⊠	ct-Shared Bed Count Surgery
⊠	ct-Shared Bed Count
⊠	Distributed Budget
⊠	Merged Budget 1
⊠	rs-Corey's Grant Budget

C **Hold down** Ctrl and click both the Distributed Budget file and the Merged Budget 1 file; then **release** Ctrl.

8. Use Ctrl+C from the keyboard to **copy** the files to the Clipboard.

9. **Scroll up**, if necessary, until the Grant Project folder is visible at the top of the file list, and then **double-click** the folder to open it.

10. Use Ctrl+V from the keyboard to **paste** the files.

11. Navigate back to the Lesson 04 folder.

12. **Select** the original three files you selected in **step 7, tap** Delete, and choose **Yes** to confirm the deletion.

13. Open the **Grant Project** folder.

14. Open the **Connections Grant Cardiology Budget** workbook file, and leave the file **open** for the next exercise.

Inserting and Viewing Comments

Excel's Comment feature is a great tool for online collaboration. A comment is a text note that you can embed inside a workbook cell without cluttering the normal view of the workbook. You may display all comments on a worksheet and even print them.

When to Use a Comment

Comments are an excellent way to handle many situations. You may want to insert a comment:

- To document the formula or value in a cell.
- To record a question about the worksheet data to be followed up later.
- To ask a question of an online collaborator without placing it into the normally printed page of the workbook.

Viewing Comments

When someone inserts a comment, Excel places a small red triangle at the top-right corner of the cell. When you point at the cell containing the red triangle, Excel displays the name of the author and the text of the comment. You also may display or hide one or all comments using commands in the Comments group on the Review Ribbon. The following illustration shows a cell and its associated comment.

Pointing at the cell containing the red triangle will pop up the comment. ⟶

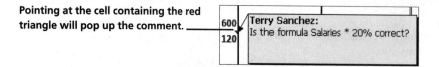

Terry Sanchez:
Is the formula Salaries * 20% correct?

Navigating Through Comments

You may jump from one comment to the next with the Next and Previous commands in the Ribbon. Using these commands is especially useful in large worksheets. When you reach the last comment in the workbook, the Next command starts over with the first comment in the workbook. The following figure displays the Comments group commands on the Ribbon.

These buttons navigate backward and forward through the comments. ⟶

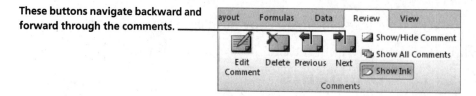

 Hands-On 4.3: Review Comments

1. Follow these steps to display some comments on the Cardiology worksheet of the Connection Grant Cardiology Budget workbook:

Ⓐ **Point at this cell containing a comment triangle and read Terry Sanchez's comment.** ⟶

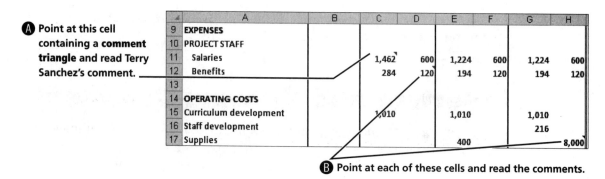

Ⓑ **Point at each of these cells and read the comments.**

2. Choose **Review→Comments→Show All Comments** 🔲 from the Ribbon.

3. Choose **Review→Comments→Show All Comments** 🔲 from the Ribbon again to toggle off the display of the comments.

4. Choose **Review→Comments→Next** 🔲 from the Ribbon

5. Repeat the **Next** command to view the second comment.

6. Choose **Review→Comments→Previous** 🔲 from the Ribbon.

7. Issue the **Next** command three times until prompted that you are at the end of the workbook.

8. Click **OK** in the Microsoft Excel dialog box to start over at the first comment.

9. Select any cell to hide the comment, and leave the workbook **open**.

Setting the Username

Before you insert comments, you should set the username to identify that the comment came from you. You make this setting in the Excel Options window in the General category. Once you set the username, Excel will keep this setting until the username is changed to something else.

Inserting and Deleting Comments

You may insert a comment into any cell with the New Comment ⬚ command on the Ribbon or by right-clicking a cell and choosing Insert Comment from the context menu. A comment is specific to a cell; you cannot assign a comment to a range of cells. You cannot insert more than one comment box in a cell, but you may add to an existing comment. After you give the command, a comment box appears in which you may type the text of the comment. Clicking outside the comment box hides it when Show All Comments is turned off. The Delete command on the Review ribbon will remove the selected comment from its cell.

FROM THE KEYBOARD
Shift + F2 to insert comment

Adding to Comments

🖊 You may add to comments made by other authors by clicking in the comment box and typing. If the comment is not displayed, you may select the cell and choose Edit Comment from the Ribbon or context menu. Typing your name in bold is recommended to identify your portion of the comment.

Example of an Edited Comment

As you read comments inserted by your co-worker in another department, you notice one that asks a question. Rather than insert a new comment, you decide to add your answer by editing the existing comment. You also may apply a different text color to this edit so that the other readers can readily distinguish your addition from the original comment.

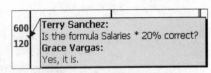

Formatting Comment Text

You may change most text attributes for your comment using commands on the Home Ribbon, but the Font Color command is not available on the Ribbon. Instead, you should use the Format Comment command in the context menu to display a dialog box, where you may change the font color.

Positioning and Sizing a Comment

A comment box may be moved by dragging its border or using the cursor keys to nudge the box. You may resize a comment box by dragging any of the eight resizing handles that appear around its edge. A comment box does not expand automatically to display all the text of a lengthy comment. You may use cursor keys to scroll through text in a comment, but resizing the comment box will ensure that everyone can read the entire comment.

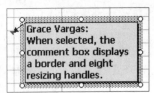

Hands-On 4.4: Insert and Add to Comments

1. Choose **File→Options** . Display the **General** category, if not already displayed.

2. Under Personalize Your Copy of Microsoft Office, notice the current **User Name**.

3. As directed by your instructor, write the current username *exactly as shown* so that you may restore that name at the end of this exercise, or write the restoration procedure in the space provided:

_____

4. Change the existing username in the User Name box to **your first name and last name**, and click **OK** to save the change.

5. Verify that the Connections Grant Cardiology Budget workbook in the Grants Project folder is **open**.

6. **Right-click** cell G20 and choose **Insert Comment** from the context menu.

7. Type the following comment in the comment box:

   Participation in the League for Innovation conference.

8. **Tap** Enter, and then select **cell G20** to close the Edit Comment box and hide your comment.

9. Point at **cell G20** to pop up your comment.

10. **Right-click** cell D12 and choose **Edit Comment** from the context menu.

11. Use Ctrl + B to turn on bold, **type** your name followed by a colon (:), **tap** Enter, and use Ctrl + B to turn off bold.

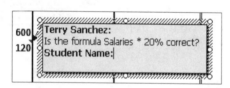

12. **Drag down** the center-bottom handle of the comment box to enlarge the box, if necessary.

13. **Right-click** anywhere in the comment text and choose **Format Comment** from the context menu.

14. In the Format Comment dialog box, drop down the **Color** list, choose a new text color, such as Blue, and then click **OK**.

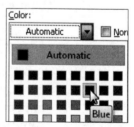

15. **Type** the following: **Yes, it is**.

16. Select **cell D12** to close the comment box.

17. **Right-click** cell D12 and choose **Show/Hide Comments** from the context menu.

18. Choose **Review→Comments→Show All Comments** from the Ribbon to display all comments.

19. Click in the **cell D12** comment box to select it.

20. Follow these steps to change the location of a comment on the worksheet:

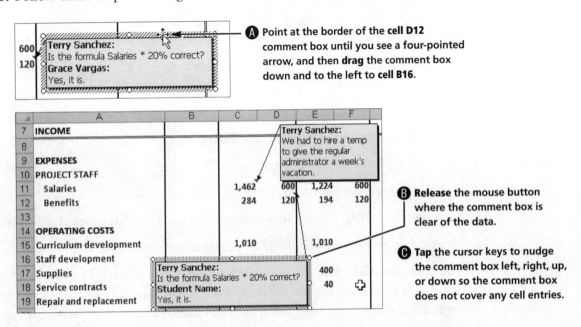

A Point at the border of the **cell D12** comment box until you see a four-pointed arrow, and then **drag** the comment box down and to the left to **cell B16**.

B **Release** the mouse button where the comment box is clear of the data.

C **Tap** the cursor keys to nudge the comment box left, right, up, or down so the comment box does not cover any cell entries.

21. Right-click cell H17 and choose **Delete Comment** from the context menu.

22. Save 🖫 the changes, and leave the workbook **open** for the next exercise. ∎

Printing Comments

Excel's default setting is to suppress the printing of comments. To print the comments in a workbook, you choose a comments printing mode in the Page Setup dialog box. You may print each currently displayed comment where it appears on the worksheet or print all comments (whether displayed or not) on a separate sheet.

Hands-On 4.5: Print Comments

1. Choose **Review→Comments→Show All Comments** 🗔 from the Ribbon to display all comments, if not already displayed.

2. Choose **Page Layout→Page Setup dialog box launcher** ▫ from the Ribbon.

3. Display the **Sheet** tab in the Page Setup dialog box.

4. Under Print, drop down the Comments list and choose **As Displayed on Sheet**.

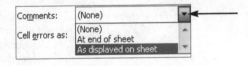

5. Click the **Print Preview** button near the bottom of the Sheet tab in the dialog box.

6. Click the **Page Setup** link at the bottom-left corner of Backstage view.

7. Display the **Sheet** tab in the Page Setup dialog box.

8. Choose **At End of Sheet** from the Comments list, and click **OK**.

9. Click the **Next Page** button at the bottom of Backstage view to display page 2.

10. Click the **Print** button at the upper-left corner of Backstage view to print the worksheet with a separate comments page.

11. Retrieve the printout from the printer.

12. Choose **Page Layout→Page Setup dialog box launcher** from the Ribbon.

13. Display the **Sheet** tab in the Page Setup dialog box.

14. Choose **(None)** from the Comments list and click **OK**.

15. **Save** the changes, and **close** the workbook. Leave Excel **open**.

16. Choose **File→Options**. Display the **General** category, if not already displayed.

17. Under **Personalize Your Copy of Microsoft Office**, carefully **type** the original username that you wrote down during Develop Your Skills 4.4 in the User Name box and click **OK**.

Preparing Workbooks for Distribution

Assume that you created a workbook and checked its contents for accuracy. You wouldn't want your colleagues or clients to make changes or view confidential information unless authorized. You can perform a few more steps to enhance data security before sharing the workbook with other people.

Inspecting Workbooks for Personal Information and Hidden Data

The Document Inspector tool can search for certain items in a workbook that you may not wish other people to see. When the Document Inspector displays the search result, you may choose to remove items from the workbook from within the search result. The removal may be permanent, and you cannot choose specific instances within a category. For example, you may choose to remove all document property types listed in the search result but not just some of them. You may, however, choose not to remove all in Document Inspector and instead delete any single item manually in the workbook as you would normally.

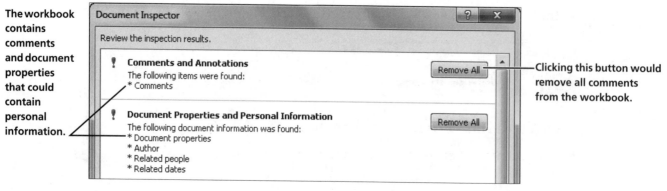

The workbook contains comments and document properties that could contain personal information.

Clicking this button would remove all comments from the workbook.

The Document Inspector report

Marking a Workbook as Final

The Mark as Final command in the Info tab of Backstage view saves the workbook and sets the file as read-only. A co-worker can view the workbook but cannot enter, change, or format data. This feature is not foolproof, though. Anyone who opens the workbook can turn off the "final" status.

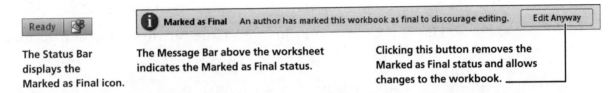

The Status Bar displays the Marked as Final icon.

The Message Bar above the worksheet indicates the Marked as Final status.

Clicking this button removes the Marked as Final status and allows changes to the workbook.

Granting a User Permission to View or Edit a Workbook

In addition to locking cells on a worksheet and protecting the workbook, you may control who may open a workbook and whether they may edit, print, or copy data from it. You also may set a permission expiration date. Your network administrator may set up rights management on your intranet server. As an alternative, you may sign up for a Windows Live account and use the free Windows Rights Management Services Client software to embed your chosen permissions and restrictions in the workbook file. When users try to open the file, they receive a message to connect to the licensing server. If the user's credentials are verified as valid, the server downloads a license to use the file and the workbook opens. Otherwise, a message indicates that the user does not have permission rights for the file.

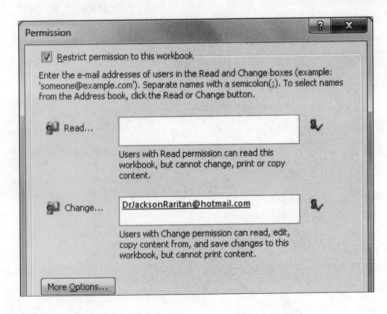

This Permission dialog box indicates that one user may open and change the workbook.

The Status Bar displays an icon to indicate that a permission policy is applied to the workbook.

Hands-On 4.6: Inspect and Mark a Workbook as Final

1. **Open** the Distributed Budget workbook from the Grant Project folder in the Lesson 04 folder.

2. Choose **File→Save As** 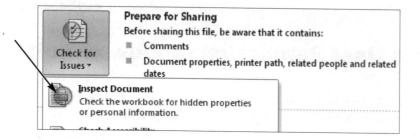, change the filename to **Distributed Budget Final**, make certain that the **Grant Projects** folder is active, and click **Save**.

3. Choose **File→Info,** and choose **Check for Issues menu ▼→Inspect Document** in the Info tab of Backstage view.

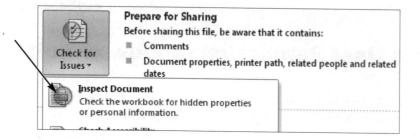

Prepare for Sharing
Before sharing this file, be aware that it contains:
- Comments
- Document properties, printer path, related people and related dates

Inspect Document
Check the workbook for hidden properties or personal information.

4. Read the inspection categories, and then click **Inspect** at the bottom of the dialog box.

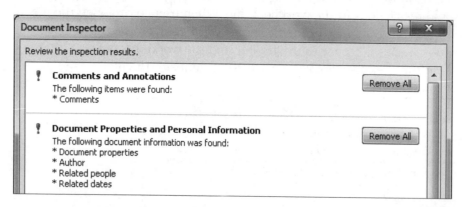

Document Inspector

Review the inspection results.

Comments and Annotations
The following items were found:
* Comments

Document Properties and Personal Information
The following document information was found:
* Document properties
* Author
* Related people
* Related dates

5. Click **Remove All** at the right of Comments and Annotations.

6. Click **Remove All** at the right of Document Properties and Personal Information.

7. Close the **Document Inspector** dialog box.

8. **Tap** Esc to exit Backstage view, and notice that all comments were removed.

Properties ▼

Size	20.0KB
Title	Add a title
Tags	Add a tag
Categories	Add a category

Related Dates

Last Modified	Today, 7:19 PM
Created	2/18/1998 4:29 PM
Last Printed	6/26/2010 4:52 PM

Related People

Author	Add an author
Last Modified By	Student Name

9. Choose **File→Info**, and choose **Protect Workbook menu ▼→Mark as Final** in the Info tab of Backstage view.

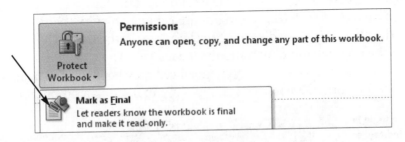

10. Read the Microsoft Excel message, and click **OK**.

11. Read another message, if one appears, and click **OK**.

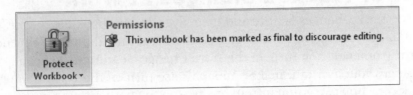

12. **Tap** [Esc] to exit Backstage view, and read the Message Bar about the workbook.

13. Select any cell in the worksheet, and attempt to enter data.

14. Click the **Edit Anyway** button in the Message Bar.

15. **Save** 💾 the changes, and **close** the workbook.

Sharing Workbooks Without a Network

In a workgroup environment, several team members may need to access the same workbook simultaneously. For example, they may be independently checking data, entering data into areas of a project workbook assigned to them, or updating rapidly changing data. You may set up a shared workbook for other users to edit. If your organization does not have a computer network available, you may distribute the shared workbook using either of the following methods:

1. Sending one copy to the first team member to make changes and then routing the same file to the next user

2. Giving each user his/her own copy in which to make changes

You will set the workbook as shared, track changes made by the various users, and review the changes. The Excel commands that you use will vary depending on the method.

Tracking Changes to Workbooks

When several people make changes to the same workbook, one person usually is assigned to review and approve each change. Excel can maintain a change history that tracks each change to the workbook. The change history displays the username of the person who made each change along with the original and new contents of each cell. The change history lets you review each change and accept or reject it. A changed cell may be identified by its border and a triangle in the upper-left corner. Each user's changes are marked in a different color.

The cell border and a triangle in the upper-left corner indicate a tracked change in this cell.

Nikki Young, , 1/16/2013 9:07 PM:
Changed cell G11 from '1,063.00' to '1650.00'.

A comment automatically records details about the change and who made it.

Example of Tracked Changes at Work

You turn on the Track Changes feature and then give the workbook file to your assistant. You ask him to contact two grant and contract specialists and then input any expenditures not yet included in the workbook. You turn on the Track Changes feature so you can quickly see and review all changes your assistant makes. You may also turn on the Track Changes feature for one workbook copy before passing it from one person to another for changes and then back to the project manager to approve the changes. Switching on Track Changes also sets that workbook to be shared. In this case, you need not also use the Share Workbook command described later in this lesson.

Hands-On 4.7: Track Changes to a Workbook

1. **Open** the Shared Budget workbook from the Grant Project folder, which is within the Lesson 04 folder in your file storage location.

2. Choose **File→Options** 📄. Display the **General** category, if not already displayed.

3. Under Personalize Your Copy of Microsoft Office, notice the name in the **User Name** box.

4. Change the existing name in the **User Name** box to your first name and last name, and click **OK**.

5. Choose **Review→Changes→Track Changes** 📝→**Highlight Changes** from the Ribbon.

6. Follow these steps to set up tracking changes:

Ⓐ Make certain that this box contains a **checkmark** to turn on tracking changes and share the workbook.

Ⓑ Make certain that the **When** option is checked. Display the **When** list, read the options, and choose **All**.

Ⓒ Place a checkmark in the **Who** box and choose **Everyone** from the list, if not already set.

Ⓓ Leave the **Where** option **unchecked** so that the entire workbook is available for tracking.

Ⓔ Make certain that this box contains a **checkmark**.

Highlight Changes

☑ T̲rack changes while editing. This also shares your workbook.

Highlight which changes

☑ Whe̲n: All

☑ Wh̲o: Everyone

☐ Whe̲re:

☑ Highlight changes on s̲creen
☐ List changes on a new sheet

7. Click **OK** to close the dialog box, and then click **OK** when prompted to save the workbook.

Shared Budget [Shared] - Microsoft Excel

8. Display the **Orthopedics Dept** worksheet.

9. Select **cell E21**, which currently has a value of 2,308, and enter **1725**.

10. **Right-click** cell E21 and choose **Insert Comment** from the context menu. Type the comment `Network server was repaired.`

11. Click **outside** the comment box.

12. Point at **cell E21** but do not click. In the pop-up box that appears, read the change history and your comment for cell E21.

13. If the comment box remains visible when you point to a different cell, choose **Review→Comments→Show All Comments** from the Ribbon to turn off the display of comments.

14. Select **cell G16** and **enter** a value of **725**.

15. Select **cell G11** and change the value to **5844**.

16. **Save** 🖫 the changes.

Reviewing Tracked Changes

You may review changes to a workbook that has the Track Changes feature switched on. When you review changes, Excel can jump from one change to the next, giving you the opportunity to accept or reject each change. After you have reviewed a change, Excel keeps a record of the change until you deactivate the Track Changes feature. The following list describes your review options.

- **Accept**—An accepted change is kept in the cell. The change history records the old value that was replaced.
- **Reject**—A rejected change restores the old value in the cell. The change history records the new value that was rejected.
- **Accept All or Reject All**—All changes that have not yet been reviewed may be rejected or accepted with a single command.

The Change History

After you have reviewed changes to a worksheet, the change history retains a copy of the reviewed cells, including their old and new values and any rejected values. Thus, even after you accept a change, you may refer to the change history and manually reinstate an old or rejected value. You may view the change history by displaying a separate History worksheet. This worksheet is deleted automatically when you save the workbook, but you may give the command again.

Hands-On 4.8: Review the Changes

1. Choose **File→Options** 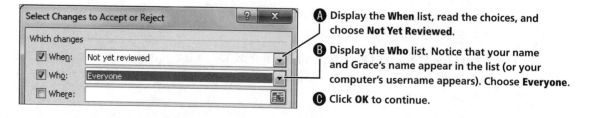. Display the **General** category, if not already displayed.

2. Under Personalize Your Copy of Microsoft Office, notice the current **User Name**.

3. Enter **Grace Vargas** in the User Name box, and click **OK** to save the change.

4. Choose **Review→Changes→Track Changes** →**Accept/Reject Changes** from the Ribbon.

5. Follow these steps to examine your choices:

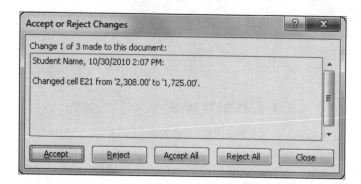

A Display the **When** list, read the choices, and choose **Not Yet Reviewed**.

B Display the **Who** list. Notice that your name and Grace's name appear in the list (or your computer's username appears). Choose **Everyone**.

C Click **OK** to continue.

6. If necessary, drag the title bar to move the **Accept or Reject Changes** dialog box so that **cell E21** is visible.

7. Point at **cell E21**, but do not click.

8. Click the **Accept** button to accept this change to the workbook.

9. Click the **Reject** button.

10. Click the **Accept** button for **cell G11**.

11. Scroll down so that **row 16** is at the top of the window.

12. Point at **cell E21**.

13. Scroll up until **row 1** is visible.

14. **Save** the workbook.

15. Choose **Review→Changes→Track Changes** →**Highlight Changes** from the Ribbon.

16. Place a checkmark in the box next to **List Changes on a New Sheet** near the bottom of the dialog box and click **OK**.

Action Number	Date	Time	Who	Change	Sheet	Range	New Value	Old Value	Action Type	Losing Action
1	5/21/2010	10:22 PM	Student Name	Cell Change	Orthopedics Dept	E21	1725	2308		
2	5/21/2010	10:22 PM	Student Name	Cell Change	Orthopedics Dept	G16	725	<blank>		
3	5/21/2010	10:22 PM	Student Name	Cell Change	Orthopedics Dept	G11	5844	1063		
4	5/21/2010	10:35 PM	Grace Vargas	Cell Change	Orthopedics Dept	G16	<blank>		Result of rejected action	2

The history ends with the changes saved on 5/21/2010 at 10:35 PM.

17. **Save** 💾 the workbook.

18. Choose **Review→Changes→Track Changes** →**Highlight Changes** from the Ribbon.

19. Remove the checkmark from the **Track Changes While Editing** box and click **OK**.

20. Click **Yes** when asked to confirm removal of the change history and workbook sharing.

21. Display the **Orthopedics Dept** worksheet.

22. **Close** the workbook, and leave Excel **open**.

23. Choose **File→Options**. Display the **General** category, if not already displayed.

24. Under **Personalize our Copy of Microsoft Office**, carefully **type** the original username you wrote down during Develop Your Skills 4.4 in the User Name box and click **OK**.

Merging Multiple Workbooks

You may choose to share a workbook by distributing a copy to each user rather than placing it on a network server. The Compare and Merge Workbooks command gives you the capability to merge the multiple copies of the workbook containing all user changes into a single workbook. This saves you the tedium of opening each workbook individually and then selecting, copying, and pasting the necessary cells into the primary workbook. The files to be merged must all be copies of the *original* workbook, and the copies must have unique file-names. For example, users may add their initials to the filename, such as mw-Budget and tg-Budget.

Example of a Merge

You create a shared workbook. You send the workbook to several people by email as an attachment and request that the recipients fill in data on specific sections. After the workbook copies are returned, you use the Compare and Merge Workbooks command to merge them into your original shared workbook. You will not have to look for, copy, and paste the data. Then, you use the Accept/Reject Changes command to resolve any changes that multiple users made to the same cell.

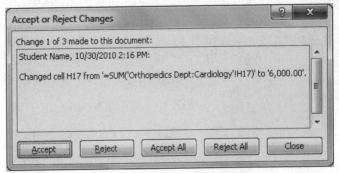

The Compare and Merge Workbooks command displays all changes made to a cell.

What Happens When Workbooks Are Merged

Excel performs several operations when you merge workbooks. The details are described in the following table.

Change	Description
Data is merged into the currently active workbook	Whichever copy of the shared workbook you have open when you give the Compare and Merge Workbooks command is the one that receives the merged data. The copies of the workbook you are merging from do not receive merged data.
Merged data replaces original data	Data merged from other workbook(s) will replace any data already existing in the same cells of the workbook into which you are merging.
A change history is recorded	Excel records all changes that occur during the merge, including where the data came from and who made the change. You may review the changes and accept any one change to a cell.

Merged Cells Compared to Merged Workbooks

Do not confuse the Compare and Merge Workbooks command with merged cells. Merged cells allow you to combine a range of cells and center a label across the cells. You cannot merge cells in a shared workbook. You must either merge cells before sharing the workbook or turn off sharing.

Protecting Elements in a Shared Workbook

 You may protect worksheet elements before setting the workbook to be shared. For example, you may lock or unlock cells and then turn on worksheet protection. The Protect and Share Workbook command sets the workbook to be shared and provides two additional protection levels. The share and track changes features are dimmed in dialog boxes to prevent users from switching them off in an individual copy of a shared workbook. You may also set a password to ensure that only designated users may alter this protection. This password is distinct from any passwords set to protect cells or worksheets.

Hands-On 4.9: Merge Two Workbooks

1. Choose **File→Options**. Display the **General** category, if not already displayed.

2. Under **Personalize Your Copy of Microsoft Office**, enter your **first and last name** in the User Name box and click **OK**.

3. **Open** the Merged Budget 1 workbook.

4. Choose **Review→Changes→Protect and Share Workbook** from the Ribbon.

5. Place a checkmark in the box next to **Sharing with Track Changes** and click **OK**.

6. Click **OK** to confirm saving the shared workbook.

7. Choose **Review→Changes→Share Workbook** from the Ribbon.

8. Click **Cancel** to exit the dialog box without making any changes.

9. Choose **File→Save As**. Change the number from 1 to **2** in the filename and click **Save**.

10. Display the **Cardiology** worksheet.

11. Select **cell H17** and enter **6000** as the new value.

12. Enter **600** in **cell H11**.

13. Enter **120** in **cell H12**.

14. **Close** the workbook and choose to **save** when you are asked to save the changes.

15. Verify that the **Compare and Merge Workbooks** ⬤ command is installed on the Quick Access toolbar. If it is not, follow these steps to install the command:

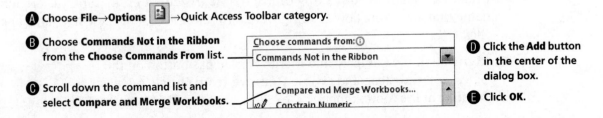

Ⓐ Choose **File→Options** 🗐 →Quick Access Toolbar category.

Ⓑ Choose **Commands Not in the Ribbon** from the **Choose Commands From** list.

Choose commands from: ⓘ
Commands Not in the Ribbon ▾

Ⓒ Scroll down the command list and select **Compare and Merge Workbooks**.

Compare and Merge Workbooks...
Constrain Numeric

Ⓓ Click the **Add** button in the center of the dialog box.

Ⓔ Click **OK.**

16. **Open** the Merged Budget 1 workbook.

17. Display the **Cardiology** worksheet.

18. Choose **Compare and Merge Workbooks** ⬤ from the Quick Access toolbar.

19. **Double-click** the Merged Budget 2 workbook to merge it into your open workbook.

20. Choose **Review→Changes→Track Changes** 📝→**Highlight Changes** from the Ribbon.

21. Follow these steps to display the change history worksheet:

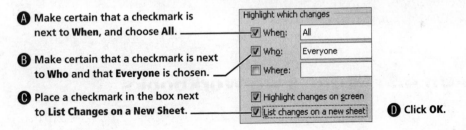

Ⓐ Make certain that a checkmark is next to **When**, and choose **All.**

Ⓑ Make certain that a checkmark is next to **Who** and that **Everyone** is chosen.

Highlight which changes
☑ When: All
☑ Who: Everyone
☐ Where:

☑ Highlight changes on screen
☑ List changes on a new sheet

Ⓒ Place a checkmark in the box next to **List Changes on a New Sheet.**

Ⓓ Click **OK.**

22. Examine **columns H and I** of the History worksheet. These columns display a new and an old value for **cell H17**.

23. Display the **Cardiology** worksheet.

24. Choose **Review→Changes→Track Changes** 📝→**Accept/Reject Changes** from the Ribbon.

25. Make certain that the dialog box is set as shown at right, and click **OK**.

26. Click **Reject** to replace 6000 with the old value.

27. Click **Accept All** to accept all remaining changes.

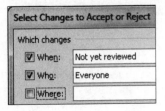

Select Changes to Accept or Reject

Which changes
☑ When: Not yet reviewed
☑ Who: Everyone
☐ Where:

28. Choose **Review→Changes→Unprotect Shared Workbook** 🗖 from the Ribbon.

29. Choose **Review→Changes→Share Workbook** 🗖 from the Ribbon.

30. On the **Editing** tab, uncheck the box next to **Allow Changes by More than One User at the Same Time**, and click **OK**.

31. Click **Yes** to confirm removing the workbook from shared use.

32. **Save** 🖫 the changes, and **close** the workbook.

33. Choose **File→Options** 🖻 and display the **General** category, if not already displayed.

34. Under **Personalize Your Copy of Microsoft Office**, carefully **type** the original username that you wrote down during Develop Your Skills 4.4 in the User Name box and click **OK**.

35. **Right-click** the Compare and Merge Workbooks button on the Quick Access toolbar, and choose **Remove from Quick Access Toolbar** in the context menu.

Concepts Review

Concepts Review labyrinthelab.com/fastcourse_excel10

To check your knowledge of the key concepts introduced in this lesson, complete the Concepts Review quiz by going to the URL listed above.

Notes

Integrating Excel with Other Programs

In this lesson, you will learn how to make Excel 2010 workbooks compatible with prior Excel versions so all project collaborators may share data. You will convert workbooks to other file formats, including PDF and XPS for document sharing. A program other than Excel may be the basis for a project. For example, you often will create reports using Word and make presentations using PowerPoint. Through the power of application integration, you may link or embed Excel data, tables, and charts in those documents. You also will bring data into Excel from external sources such as a plain-text file or Word document. Documents often are shared electronically as web pages. You will learn how to save an entire workbook as a web page, as well as save a single worksheet and selected elements from a sheet.

LESSON TIMING

- Concepts/Hands-On: 1 hr 30 min
- Concepts Review: 15 min
- Total: 1 hr 45 min

LEARNING OBJECTIVES

After studying this lesson, you will be able to:

- Save workbooks for use with prior Excel versions
- Convert workbooks to text, PDF, and XPS file formats
- Share Excel data with Word, Power-Point, and Access
- Import text and data from external sources into Excel workbooks
- Save workbook elements as a web page

CASE STUDY: PRODUCING AN ANNUAL REPORT

Deion Jenett is administrative assistant to Dr. Edward Jackson, the COO at Raritan Clinic East. Deion is halfway through a project to produce Raritan's annual report. He coordinates the efforts of the production team to get parts of the publication ready for printing and publishing to the clinic's website. Deion assembles information about the production tasks and the schedule into an Excel workbook and then publishes the workbook in a universal file format. Deion also merges Excel workbook data into forms or letters addressed to multiple recipients.

Maintaining Compatibility with Previous Versions of Excel

You can open and work with Excel workbooks saved in Excel 2010 or earlier versions such as Excel 97, 2000, 2003, and 2007. At times, you will need to share your workbooks and templates with others who have one of the earlier Excel versions or may not have Excel installed. You must ensure that files are saved in a format that those users can open.

About File Formats

A file format is a structure for storing data in a computer file. An application program uses specific file formats to save anything that you create in that program. The format that an application program normally uses to save files is called its *native* file format. For example, Word saves files using the format Word Document (.docx), and a web page editor may use the HTML file format.

Identifying a File's Format

When you give Excel's Save As ⊞ command, you may choose from a number of file formats in the Save As Type list in the Save As dialog box. The default is Excel Workbook. While browsing filenames in Excel or Windows Explorer, you may identify files that are compatible with Excel by viewing the icons next to the filenames. You may also read the extension at the end of the filename, if extensions are displayed. For example, the extension .xls indicates a spreadsheet workbook saved for use with a previous Excel version.

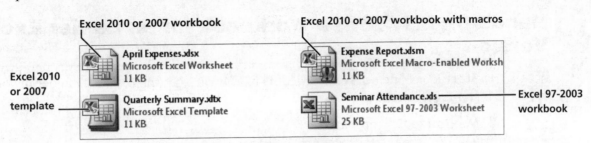

The file's icon and extension in the filename identify the file type

The following table shows the file formats that you may use to save workbooks for various Excel versions along with their file extensions.

File Type	Excel Version	Description	File Extension
Excel Workbook	2010 or 2007	Workbooks without macros	.xlsx
Excel Macro-Enabled Workbook	2010 or 2007	Workbooks with macros	.xlsm
Excel Template	2010 or 2007	Template workbooks without macros	.xltx
Excel Macro-Enabled Template	2010 or 2007	Template workbooks with macros	.xltm
Excel 97-2003 Workbook	97–2003	Workbooks with or without macros	.xls
Excel 97-2003 Template	97–2003	Template workbooks with or without macros	.xlt
Excel Binary Workbook	97–2007	Non-XML workbooks	.xlsb
Microsoft Excel 5.0/95 Workbook	95	Early-version workbooks	.xls

Excel 2010 Open XML File Formats

As you can see from the preceding table, Excel 2010 has more file formats than most previous versions to help identify files containing macros and reduce the file size, which is beneficial when you share files. The file structure, called Open XML, is based on the Extensible Markup Language (XML) used by software developers. XML is is one standard for the exchange of structured data on the Internet.

Earlier Excel File Formats

Versions prior to Excel 2010 and 2007 use different file formats than XML. For this reason, some Excel 2010 and 2007 features are not viewable in the earlier versions. Files saved in these formats display the words *[Compatibility Mode]* in the Excel title bar as shown in the following illustration.

Schedule [Compatibility Mode] - Microsoft Excel

You have the following two options to enable users of earlier versions to open and work with your Excel 2010 file.

- **Save in a Non-XML File Format**—You may save your workbook in a file format that removes the incompatible features.
- **Use the Compatibility Pack**—Users may download and install a file converter that hides the incompatible features.

Hands-On 5.1: Save a Workbook for an Earlier Excel Version

1. **Start** Excel and **open** the Schedule workbook from the Lesson 05 folder in your file storage location.

2. **Maximize** ☐ the window.

3. Choose **File→Save As** 🖫.

4. Follow these steps to save the workbook in Excel 97–2003 file format:

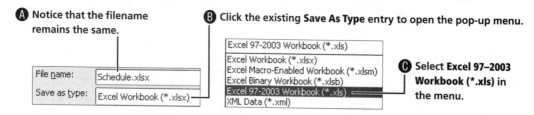

Ⓐ Notice that the filename remains the same.

Ⓑ Click the existing **Save As Type** entry to open the pop-up menu.

Ⓒ Select **Excel 97–2003 Workbook (*.xls)** in the menu.

| File name: | Schedule.xlsx |
| Save as type: | Excel Workbook (*.xlsx) |

Excel 97-2003 Workbook (*.xls)
Excel Workbook (*.xlsx)
Excel Macro-Enabled Workbook (*.xlsm)
Excel Binary Workbook (*.xlsb)
Excel 97-2003 Workbook (*.xls)
XML Data (*.xml)

5. Click **Save**.

6. Choose **File→Open** 📂, and navigate to the Lesson 05 folder, if not already displayed.

7. Follow these steps to display details about the files in the folder:

A Click the **Views menu ▾** button on the dialog box Menu Bar, and choose **Details** from the menu.

B Point at the border at the right of the **Type** column heading until the pointer resembles a double-pointed arrow. **Double-click** the border to widen the Type column. (Drag the border to the right if you have trouble double-clicking.)

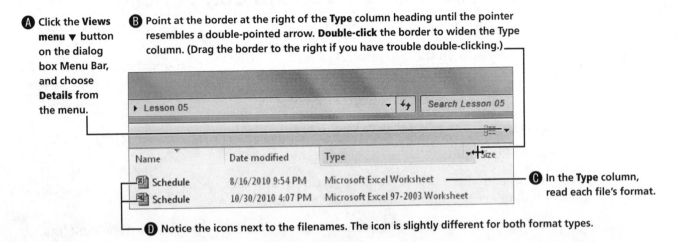

C In the **Type** column, read each file's format.

D Notice the icons next to the filenames. The icon is slightly different for both format types.

8. Click **Cancel** to exit the Open dialog box.

9. Close the workbook, and leave Excel **open**.

Checking for Excel Version Compatibility

The Compatibility Checker scans your workbook and identifies any features that would not be included if you were to save the workbook in a non-XML (nonnative) file format. The report summarizes various incompatibilities as significant or minor, and it provides a Find button to help you locate each occurrence in the workbook. You may decide to proceed if the compatibility check reports only a minor loss of fidelity, such as table formatting. Significant issues usually must be resolved. The dialog box contains an option that, when switched on, will check for compatibility every time the workbook is saved.

Check for Issues ▾

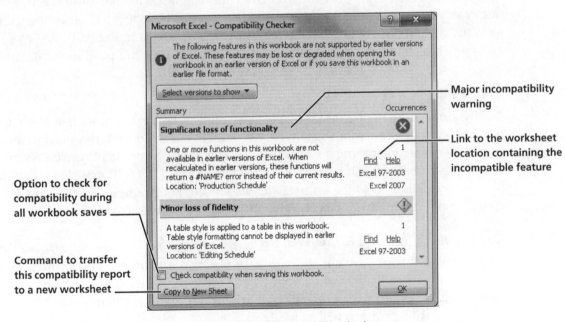

Major incompatibility warning

Link to the worksheet location containing the incompatible feature

Option to check for compatibility during all workbook saves

Command to transfer this compatibility report to a new worksheet

A report displayed by the Compatibility Checker before or while a file is saved

Hands-On 5.2: Check Excel Version Compatibility

1. **Open** the Compatibility Check workbook from the Lesson 05 folder.

2. Choose **File→Info**. In the Info tab of Backstage view, choose **Check for Issues menu ▾**, and choose **Check Compatibility**.

3. **Scroll** through the window and read both messages.

4. Click the **Help** link under Minor Loss of Fidelity.

5. **Close** the Help window.

6. In the Compatibility Checker window, **scroll up** and click the **Find** link under Significant Loss of Functionality.

7. Notice that the Compatibility Checker window is closed because you used the Find link.

8. Choose **File→Save As** 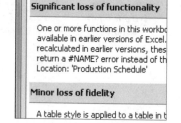.

9. In the Save As dialog box, drop down the **Save As Type** list, and choose **Excel 97-2003 Workbook**.

10. Click **Save**.

11. Click **Copy to New Sheet**.

12. **Close** the workbook without saving again.

Using the Compatibility Pack

A free compatibility download from Microsoft allows users of previous Excel 2000, XP (2002), and 2003 versions to open and work with Excel 2010 files. Users are prompted to download and install the Microsoft Office Compatibility Pack the first time they attempt to open an Excel 2010 file. Thereafter, any opened Excel 2010 files will be converted automatically. Any formatting or other features specific to Excel 2010 do not display when the file is opened in the previous version but are preserved when the file is reopened in Excel 2010. Having that capability may be worth asking other users to take the time to install the Compatibility Pack.

Converters

A converter is a small program that allows an application program such as Excel to open files that are not in the program's native file format. For example, you may need to import data from a Word document into a worksheet. Excel features a variety of converters that are installed automatically. You also may download and install additional converters that may become available as new file formats are introduced. For example, when a new version of an application program is released, it often introduces a new native file format.

Example of Using a Converter

You send a workbook saved in an Excel 2010 file format to another user who uses Excel 2003. The other user installs the Compatibility Pack, which includes converter programs. When she opens your Excel 2010 file, it is converted to a format that is compatible with her Excel version. Any incompatible features will be hidden.

Converting Workbooks to Other File Formats

At times, you may need to save worksheet data to use in a program other than Excel or upload a worksheet onto a web page. You may choose from several file formats in the Save As dialog box, such as XML Data or Web Page. This topic explains two common methods of sharing data between incompatible programs or with users who do not have the original program.

Text File Formats

Text file formats are commonly used to export data to or from another program that is incompatible with Excel. All worksheet formatting, such as fonts, colors, and graphics, is removed. Two types of text files are used most often in conjunction with Excel: comma delimited and tab delimited.

Comma Delimited

A comma delimited text file uses a comma to separate two columns of data. The following illustration shows an example of Excel data converted in a comma delimited file. When saving a workbook in this file format, you would choose CSV (Comma Delimited) from the Save As Type list. The filename extension .csv is added to the filename.

```
First,Last,Phone,City
Deion,Jenett,619-555-7823,San Diego
Jacqueline,Chan,303-555-8989,Denver
Jason,Stevens,540-555-2220,Bristol
```
Excel column data converted to the comma delimited format

Tab Delimited

A tab delimited file uses a tab character to separate two columns of data. In the following example of a tab delimited file, each small arrow represents a non-printing tab code. When saving a workbook in this file format, you would choose Text (Tab Delimited) from the Save As Type list. The filename extension .txt is added to the filename.

First →	Last →	Phone →	City
Deion →	Jenett →	619-555-7823 →	San Diego
Jacqueline →	Chan →	303-555-8989 →	Denver
Jason →	Stevens →	540-555-2220 →	Bristol

Excel column data converted to the tab delimited format

Limitations of File Formats

Some file formats will not save all information in the workbook file. For example, a tab delimited file won't save data on multiple worksheets or any cell formatting. Excel will warn you about features, formatting, or data you might lose in the new file format. When you save a workbook to a non-Excel file format, a second file is created. The original workbook file is not changed.

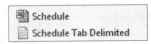

Icons and filenames for an original Excel workbook and a version saved in tab delimited format

Example of a File Format Limitation

You decide to convert a workbook to tab delimited format. Excel warns you that only the currently selected worksheet can be saved to the new file. So, you perform a save command for each worksheet in the workbook. Now each worksheet is contained in a separate file. You also notice that comments on the worksheets are not saved in the tab delimited format.

Hands-On 5.3: Convert Excel Data to Text

1. **Open** the original Schedule workbook that is in the Excel Workbook file format. Its icon is shown to the right. Display the **Details** view to determine the correct file in the Save As dialog box, if necessary.

2. Display the **Editing Schedule** worksheet, if not already displayed.

3. Choose **File→Save As** 🔳.

4. Follow these steps to save the workbook in the tab delimited file format:

Ⓐ Display the **Save As Type** list, scroll down, and choose **Text (Tab Delimited)**.

File name: Schedule Tab Delimited

Save as type: Text (Tab delimited) (*.txt)

Ⓑ Add **Tab Delimited** to the end of the filename.

5. Click the **Save** button and read the warning box.

6. Click **OK** to acknowledge the warning, and then review the next warning box that appears.

7. Choose **Yes** to continue the conversion to the tab delimited format.

8. Use Ctrl + W to close the workbook. Choose **not** to save when you are asked if you wish to save the workbook.

9. Choose **File→Open** 📂 and navigate to the Lesson 05 folder, if necessary.

10. Choose **Text Files** from the Files of Type list, as shown below. Your dialog box may differ depending on your Windows version.

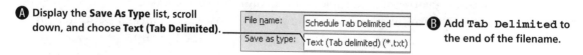

File name: Text Files

11. Follow these steps to open the text file in Notepad:

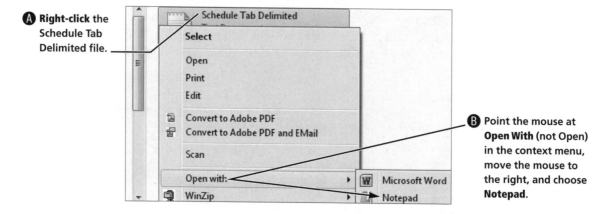

Ⓐ **Right-click** the Schedule Tab Delimited file.

Schedule Tab Delimited

Select

Open
Print
Edit

Convert to Adobe PDF
Convert to Adobe PDF and EMail

Scan

Open with: ▶   Ⓦ Microsoft Word

WinZip   ▶   Notepad

Ⓑ Point the mouse at **Open With** (not Open) in the context menu, move the mouse to the right, and choose **Notepad**.

12. **Close** the Notepad window. Choose **not** to save if you are asked to save changes to the file.

13. **Cancel** Excel's Open dialog box.

PDF and XPS File Formats

The PDF (Portable Document Format) and XPS (XML Paper Specification) file formats may be applied to Excel workbooks and many other types of documents. These file formats allow colleagues to view and print a workbook with all formatting intact even if they don't have any Excel version, and it also prevents them from making any changes or accessing any hidden information. For example, a user who installs the free Adobe Acrobat Reader may view a PDF document. You may use either the Save As command in the File tab or the Create PDF/XPS command in the Save & Send tab of Backstage view to publish the document. You may publish a selected range, a worksheet, or the entire workbook.

 ## Hands-On 5.4: Publish Excel Data as a PDF Document

1. **Open** the original Schedule workbook. Its icon is shown to the right. If necessary, change Files of Type to Excel Files to see the filename.

Schedule
Microsoft Excel Worksheet
11 KB

2. Choose **File→Save As** , and choose **PDF** in the Save As Type list.

3. Click the **Options** button near the lower-left corner of the dialog box.

4. Under **Publish What** in the Options dialog box, choose **Entire Workbook**.

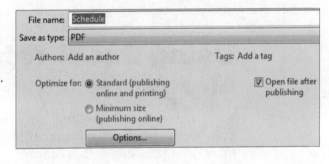

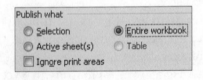

5. Click **OK**.

6. Click the **Save** button in the Save As dialog box.

7. **Maximize** the PDF reader window.

8. Use the following tools to browse through the document (your reader window may differ from the one shown):

Ⓐ If the worksheet is not readable, click the **decrease magnification** button or **increase magnification** button multiple times until it is readable. ⎯⎯⎯⎯⎯⎯

Ⓑ Click the **Next Page** button to view page 2. Click **again** to view page 3.

9. Close the reader window.

10. Close the Schedule workbook, and leave Excel **open**. Choose **not** to save if you are asked to save.

Using Excel Tables with Word Mail Merge

You may wish to send multiple customers a letter or an envelope containing marketing materials. Word's mail merge feature helps you prepare a standard message (called the main document) and personalize each copy with the customer's name, address, most recent order date, and other data unique to that customer. You may use a list or table from an Excel worksheet as a data source for these and other documents in Word. In this lesson, you will work with tables. A table should be set up with each field (column) containing one type of data, such as the order date. You insert various field names in the main document to personalize the message. When the mail merge is completed, data from each record (row) of the data source replace the field names, and you have a personalized document copy for each record.

Hands-On 5.5: Mail Merge Excel Table Data in Word

1. Open the Employee List workbook from the Lesson 05 folder in your file storage location. If necessary, change Files of Type to **All Excel Files** to see the filename in the Open dialog box.

2. Display the **Orthopedics** worksheet.

3. Close the workbook.

4. Start **Word** and **open** Seminar Form from the Lesson 05 folder.

5. Choose **Mailings→Start Mail Merge→Start Mail Merge** 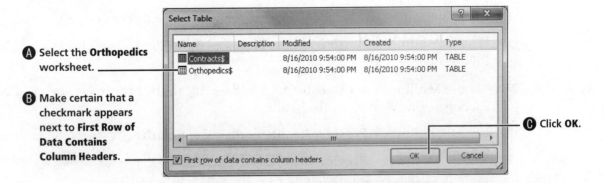 from the Ribbon.

6. **Press** Esc to cancel the menu.

7. Choose **Mailings→Start Mail Merge→Select Recipients** →**Use Existing List** from the Ribbon.

8. In the **Select Data Source** dialog box, navigate to the Lesson 05 folder in your file storage location, choose the Employee List workbook, click **Open**, and confirm the **data source**.

9. Follow these steps to select the Orthopedics worksheet:

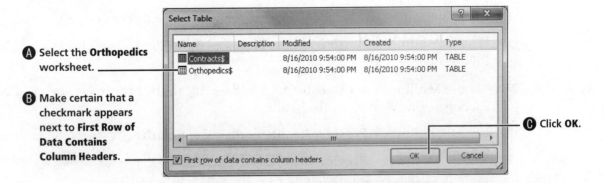

A Select the **Orthopedics** worksheet.

B Make certain that a checkmark appears next to **First Row of Data Contains Column Headers**.

C Click **OK**.

10. Choose **Mailings→Start Mail Merge→Edit Recipient List** 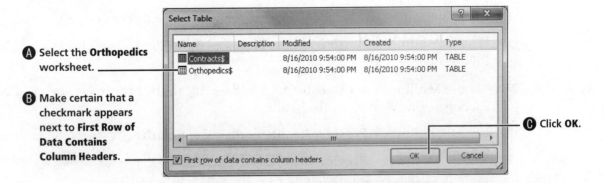 from the Ribbon.

11. In the **Mail Merge Recipients** dialog box, click in the checkbox next to employees Gonzalez, Howard, and Lawrence to deselect the department's physicians and department chief.

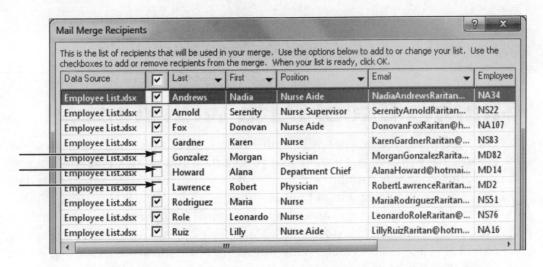

12. Click **OK** in the Mail Merge Recipients dialog box.

13. **Click** in the blank to the right of Employee Name in the form.

14. Choose **Mailings→Write & Insert Fields→Insert Merge Field** menu ▾→**First** from the Ribbon, and then **tap** Spacebar.

15. Choose **Mailings→Write & Insert Fields→Insert Merge Field** menu ▾→**Last** from the Ribbon.

16. Use the preceding step to add the **Employee ID** and **Position** fields as shown in the following illustration.

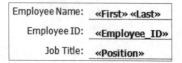

17. **Click** in the blank to the right of Dept. Head and type **Alana Howard, MD**.

Dept. Head: Alana Howard, MD

18. **Click** in the blank to the right of Department and type **Orthopedics**.

19. Choose **Mailings→Write & Insert Fields→Highlight Merge Fields** from the Ribbon.

20. Choose **Mailings→Write & Insert Fields→Highlight Merge Fields** from the Ribbon again to toggle off the highlighting.

21. Choose **Mailings→Preview Results→Preview Results** from the Ribbon.

22. Choose **Mailings→Preview Results→Next Record** in the Ribbon. Click the button again to view the next few records.

23. Choose **Mailings→Finish→Finish and Merge →Print Documents** from the Ribbon.

24. In the Merge to Printer dialog box, choose **Current Record** and click **OK**.

25. Click **OK** in the Print dialog box to print one copy of the form.

26. Retrieve the printout from the printer.

27. **Save** the changes, and exit **Word**.

Sharing Excel Data with Access

Access, a software application in Microsoft Office, stores data in tables that look similar to Excel worksheets. While you usually may format data and create calculations more easily in Excel, the database capabilities of Access allow you to filter large amounts of data using queries and to combine data from multiple sources to create various reports. When you import an Excel worksheet into a new Access table, you have the option to link the data. Then, any updates made to the original worksheet data in Excel are shown when you reopen the database and the related Access table. Without linking, the data is not updated in Access. Linked data cannot be edited in Access.

Hands-On 5.6: Import Worksheet Data into Access

1. Start **Access**.

2. Click **Open** on the File tab, navigate to the Lesson 05 folder, and **open** the Raritan Employees database.

3. If a security warning appears above the database, click **Enable Content**.

4. Choose **External Data→Import & Link→Excel** 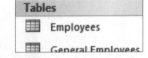 from the Ribbon.

5. In the Get External Data – Excel Spreadsheet dialog box, click **Browse** and choose the **Nurse Aides** workbook from the Lesson 05 folder.

6. Make certain that the **Import the Source Data into a New Table in the Current Database** option is selected, and then click **OK**.

7. Place a checkmark in the box next to **First Row Contains Column Headings**.

	Nurse Aide ID	Last Name	First Name
1			
2	NA1	Hardy	Brenda B.

8. Click **Next** and review the options.

9. Click **Next**, review the options, and click **Next** again.

10. In the **Import to Table** box, change the existing name to `Employees`.

11. Click **Finish**, and click **Close** in the next window. (Do not select the Save Import Steps option.)

12. **Double-click** Employees to open the table.

13. Choose **External Data→Import→Excel** 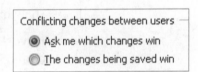 from the Ribbon.

Tables

▦ Employees

▦ General Employees

14. In the Get External Data – Excel Spreadsheet dialog box, click **Browse** and choose the **Nurse Aides** workbook.

15. Choose **Link to the Data Source by Creating a Linked Table** and click **OK**.

16. Place a checkmark in the box next to **First Row Contains Column Headings**.

17. Click **Next**.

18. Leave the Linked Table Name as **Nurse Aides**, and then click **Finish**. Click **OK** when alerted that the link has been completed.

Conflicting changes between users
◉ Ask me which changes win
◯ The changes being saved win

19. **Double-click** Nurse Aides in the Navigation Pane to open the table.

20. **Click** in any cell and try to type a different entry.

21. **Exit** ⊠ Access. Click **Yes** if prompted to save the table design.

Inserting Excel Charts in PowerPoint

Using the Paste command is usually the best method for inserting an existing Excel chart in PowerPoint. If no chart yet exists, you may create one entirely in PowerPoint using the same commands and options as in Excel, as long as Excel is installed on the same computer.

Linking Compared to Embedding

You may choose to paste a chart by converting the chart to a picture, embedding, or linking. The embedding and linking options are more useful because you can edit the chart data. Embedding places a standalone copy of the chart in the destination document. Sharing the PowerPoint presentation is simplified because the original workbook need not be distributed with the presentation. Any changes to the workbook, however, are not updated in the document holding the embedded copy. Linking a chart means that if the worksheet data is updated and saved, the chart automatically updates in the PowerPoint presentation. When you choose to paste, the embedding and linking options also allow you convert the chart to the theme of the destination document or retain the original colors and fonts.

The Paste menu with options to embed, link, or convert the chart to a picture

Hands-On 5.7: Link a Chart in PowerPoint

1. **Open** the AR Project Expenses workbook.

2. **Right-click** in a blank area of the chart and choose **Copy** from the context menu.

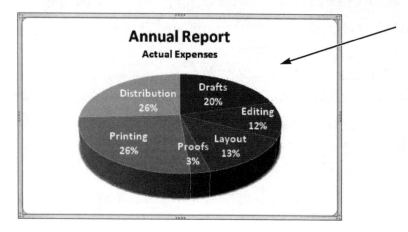

3. Leave the workbook **open**.

4. Start **PowerPoint** and open the Project Budget presentation from the Lesson 05 folder.

5. Select **slide 2 in** the Slides tab at the left of the window.

6. Follow these steps to paste the chart on slide 2:

Ⓐ In the Slide Pane, **right-click** in a blank area within the content placeholder to display the context menu.

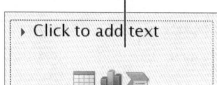

Ⓑ In the context menu, point to each button under Paste Options to read its ScreenTip. Choose **Use Destination Theme & Link Data**.

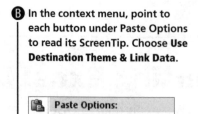

7. **Close** ⊠ Excel and leave PowerPoint **open**.

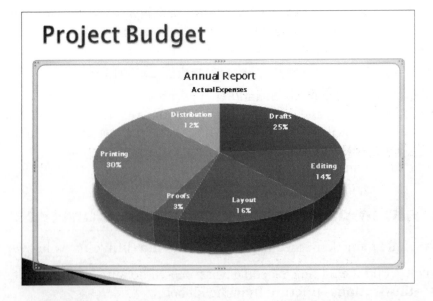

8. **Right-click** anywhere on the chart and choose **Edit Data** from the context menu.

9. In **cell D14**, notice that Distribution is 12 percent of the total expenses. Scroll to the **right**, if necessary, to see that 12 percent is also shown in the Distribution pie slice.

10. Change **cell C14** to **1000**.

11. **Close** the workbook and choose to **save** when asked if you want to save.

12. **Close** PowerPoint and choose to **save** when asked if you want to save.

Importing External Data

You can bring data from other application programs into Excel. This is called *importing*. For example, if a coworker types some information in Word, you may import this data directly into an Excel worksheet. Excel can import a variety of data into your workbooks. You may import data from as many sources as needed to complete a document. Converters are installed in Excel to import data from many popular applications.

The three methods that you may use to import data into an Excel worksheet are the following:

- **Copy and Paste**—You may use standard copy and paste commands to bring text, images, and charts into a worksheet.

- **Drag and Drop**—You may select data in another application program, use the mouse to drag the selection into an Excel worksheet, and release the mouse button.

- **Import a File**—The Get External Data command on the Data ribbon is used to import an entire text file, Access table, web page table, or data from other sources such as a network server.

Using Copy and Paste

You may copy and paste data between another application and an Excel workbook. For example, you may copy and paste a table or text from a Word document into an Excel work-sheet. You simply select the data in the other document window, cut or copy the selection, and paste it into the desired cell in the Excel window. You may also use the Paste Special command to paste data, such as images, into Excel in a specific format.

Importing Data with Drag and Drop

You may drag and drop data between another application window and an Excel workbook. For example, you may drag and drop a table or text from a Word document into an Excel worksheet. You select the data to be imported and then drag and drop it onto the desired worksheet. When you use this technique, the data is cut from the source file. However, if you then close the source file without saving, the original data will be retained.

 Hands-On 5.8: Import Data between Documents

1. **Open** the AR Production Schedule workbook and **maximize** the window.

2. Select **cell A1** on the Editing Schedule worksheet, if not already selected, and then choose **Insert→Illustrations→Picture** from the Ribbon.

3. Navigate to the Lesson 05 folder in your file storage location, if not already displayed.

4. **Double-click** Raritan Clinic Logo to insert the image in **cell A1**.

5. With the image still selected, choose **Format→Size→Shape Height**, type **.64**, and **tap** Enter .

6. **Right-click** the image and choose **Copy** from the context menu.

7. Display the **Layout Schedule** worksheet.

8. **Right-click** cell A1 and choose **Paste** from the context menu.

9. Display the **Production Schedule** worksheet and paste the logo into **cell A1**.

10. Display the **Layout Schedule** worksheet.

11. Start **Word** and **open** the AR Layout Schedule document.

12. **Right-click** in a blank area of the Windows taskbar at the bottom of the screen and choose **Show Windows Side by Side** (or **Tile Windows Vertically,** depending on your Windows version) from the context menu.

13. Click the **AR Layout Schedule** button in the Windows taskbar to activate the Word document.

14. Follow these steps to drag and drop text into the worksheet:

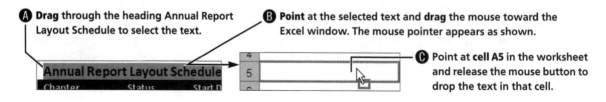

Ⓐ **Drag** through the heading Annual Report Layout Schedule to select the text.

Ⓑ **Point** at the selected text and **drag** the mouse toward the Excel window. The mouse pointer appears as shown.

Ⓒ Point at cell **A5** in the worksheet and release the mouse button to drop the text in that cell.

15. In the Excel window, **click** the first navigation button on the workbook tabs toolbar at the lower left of the window to display and select the Editing Schedule tab, as shown to the right.

16. Use the **Format Painter** 🖌 on the Ribbon to copy the formatting from **cell A5** in the Editing Schedule worksheet to **cell A5** that you just added in the Layout Schedule worksheet.

17. **Maximize** the Word window.

18. Follow these steps to copy the Word table and legend text:

Ⓐ **Point** to the left of the word *Chapter* outside the table and **drag** straight down to select the table and the Key legend text.

Ⓑ Use Ctrl+C to copy the selection.

Chapter	Status	Start Date	Due Date
1—A Message from the CEO	þ	Aug 2	Aug 3
2—Our Stories	þ	Aug 3	Aug 6
3—New Advances	x	Aug 6	Aug 7
4—Program Activities	x	Aug 8	Aug 13
5—Raritan Clinic Foundation	x	Aug 13	Aug 16
6—Financials	o	Aug 18	Aug 20
7—Board of Directions	o	Aug 21	Aug 24

Key   þ Done
x In Progress
o Awaiting Manuscript

19. Switch to the **Excel** window in the Windows taskbar.

20. **Maximize** the Excel window.

21. Select **cell A7** in the Layout Schedule worksheet, and then use Ctrl+V to paste.

22. Format the **range A7 through D18** in Calibri font and a font size of 11.

23. **Deselect** the range.

24. Widen **column A** to display all the text in the **range A8:A14**, if necessary.

25. **Right-align** the Start Date and Due Date labels over their numbers.

26. **Close** Word and choose **not** to save when asked if you want to save.

27. **Save** 💾 the changes in Excel, and leave the workbook **open**.

	A	B	C	D
1	Raritan Clinic East			
2				
3	Pediatric Diagnostic Specialists			
4				
5	Annual Report Layout Schedule			
6				
7	Chapter	Status	Start Date	Due Date
8	1—A Message from the CEO	þ	2-Aug	3-Aug
9	2—Our Stories	þ	3-Aug	6-Aug
10	3—New Advances	x	6-Aug	7-Aug
11	4—Program Activities	x	8-Aug	13-Aug
12	5—Raritan Clinic Foundation	x	13-Aug	16-Aug
13	6—Financials	o	18-Aug	20-Aug
14	7—Board of Directors	o	21-Aug	24-Aug
15				
16	Key	þ Done		
17		x In Progress		
18		o Awaiting Manuscript		

Importing a Text File

The From Text 📄 command imports an entire text file into an Excel worksheet as data. The source file format may be either tab delimited (.txt) or comma delimited (.csv). When another program is not compatible with Excel, you may need to save its data as text in one of those two formats. When you import a text file, Excel examines the file to determine whether the formatting in the file will help lay out the data neatly into rows and columns. For example, if the text file is comma delimited, Excel will place each data item following a comma in a separate column. The From Text command can also help you deal with certain formatting problems that you may encounter with tab delimited or comma delimited text files.

Hands-On 5.9: Import Data from a Text File

1. Display the **Editing Schedule** worksheet of the AR Production Schedule workbook.

2. If a warning appears above the worksheet (or in a dialog box), read the warning and click **Enable Content** (or **OK**) to confirm that you trust the website source.

3. Choose **Data→Get External Data→From Text** from the Ribbon.

4. Navigate to the Lesson 05 folder, if necessary.

5. Select the Schedule Tab Delimited text file and click **Import**.

6. In the preview of the text file in the lower portion of the dialog box, scroll until **row 7** is visible.

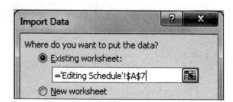

7. In the **Start Import at Row** box, enter **7** as shown to the right.

8. Click the **Next** button.

9. Scroll in the **Data Preview** section to see that text displays correctly in columns.

10. Click **Next** to continue with step 3 of the wizard.

11. Read the description of **General** format in the upper-right area of the dialog box.

12. Click **Finish** to display the Import Data dialog box.

13. Select **cell A7** in the Editing Schedule worksheet, and click **OK**.

14. Select the **range A7:C7** and add bold and a bottom border.

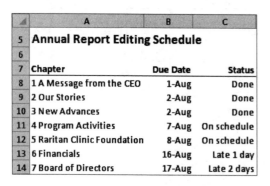

15. Add any other formatting that you think will make the text easier to read.

16. **Save** the changes, and leave the workbook **open**.

Converting Text to Columns

The Text to Columns command allows you to split cell entries on a worksheet into multiple columns. For example, cells containing a full employee name may be split into two columns for first name and last name. Cells containing the city and state may be split into two columns. The Convert Text to Columns wizard operates in a similar way to the Text Import Wizard you use to import a text file. You may split text by specifying a delimiter, such as a comma (,) or a space. You also may specify a column width. In the following illustration to the left, column A contains the chapter number and chapter name separated by a space. In the illustration below and to the right, the text has been split into columns A and B.

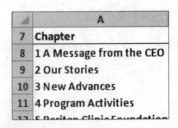

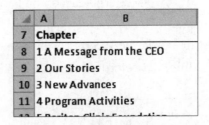

Text in a single column...   ...may be split into multiple columns.

Hands-On 5.10: Convert Text to Columns

1. Insert a blank column at **column B**.

2. Select **cell A7** in the Editing Schedule worksheet.

3. Follow these steps to add a space before the word *Chapter*:

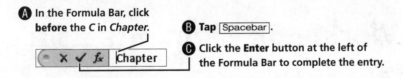

A In the Formula Bar, click **before** the C in *Chapter*.

B Tap [Spacebar].

C Click the **Enter** button at the left of the Formula Bar to complete the entry.

4. Select the **range A7:A14**.

5. Choose **Data→Data Tools→Text to Columns** from the Ribbon.

6. Click **Next**.

7. **Scroll down** in the Data Preview section until **row 5** is visible.

8. **Drag** the column break line from 20 to the right until it displays just to the right of *Foundation*.

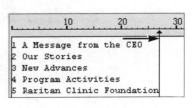

9. Click **Next** to continue with step 3 of the wizard.

10. Leave the column data format set to General, and notice that the destination cell is **A7** in the dialog box.

11. Click **Finish**; click **OK** when asked if you wish to replace the contents of the destination cell.

12. Point at the border between the column headings for **columns A and B**, and drag to the left to decrease the **column A** width.

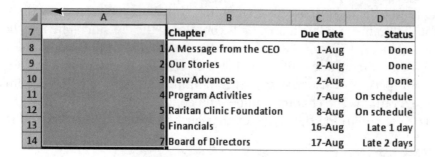

13. **Double-click** the border between the column headings for **columns B and C** to autofit the column B width.

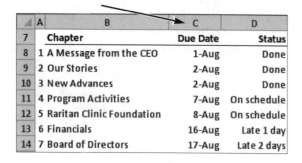

14. **Save** 💾 the changes, and **close** the workbook.

Saving Workbook Elements as a Web Page

You may save a worksheet range, an entire worksheet, or a workbook with multiple sheets as a page that users may view on the web or your organization's intranet. They cannot edit the Excel data or view formulas, and some formatting may be lost when you save as a web page. You may save as either a web page with components stored in separate files or as a single web page.

Saving as a Web Page

The Web Page option in the Save As Type list creates a main document with the filename extension .htm in the HTML (Hypertext Markup Language) format. Excel also creates a destination folder and saves workbook elements as files in that folder. You then can access individual items. For example, you may wish to replace one picture file in the folder rather than revise and republish the entire web page. You must copy both the main document and the folder to your web server.

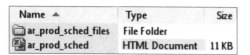

Saving an Excel workbook as a web page results in one main document and a folder containing files necessary to display the web page.

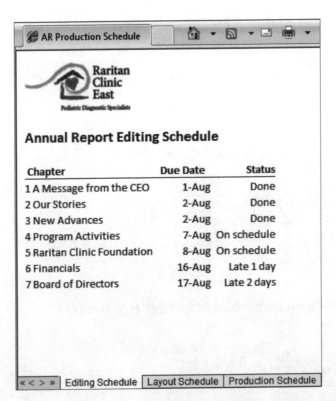

Annual Report Editing Schedule

Chapter	Due Date	Status
1 A Message from the CEO	1-Aug	Done
2 Our Stories	2-Aug	Done
3 New Advances	2-Aug	Done
4 Program Activities	7-Aug	On schedule
5 Raritan Clinic Foundation	8-Aug	On schedule
6 Financials	16-Aug	Late 1 day
7 Board of Directors	17-Aug	Late 2 days

The web page as viewed in a browser

Saving as a Single File Web Page

The Single File Web Page option in the Save As Type list is used to save all the web page elements in one file. The file is created with the filename extension .mht using the Web Archive file format. This method is useful for sending a web page as an email attachment for collaboration with others. The Web Archive file format has several limitations. A significantly larger file size results because all elements are embedded in a single file. Also, a web developer cannot edit the HTML code to update the page, and not all web browsers can open an MHT file.

Publishing the Web Page

You must publish, or upload, your document to a web server. Your network administrator may set up a destination folder on the server for you. You may publish the web page as you save it, or you may upload it later. The Save As dialog box contains options to select the workbook portion to be saved and publish the web page. You may add a page title that would be displayed in the tab of the user's web browser. You may publish first to a drive on your computer and preview how the web page looks before uploading to a web server.

Hands-On 5.11: Save a Worksheet as a Single File Web Page

1. **Open** the ar_prod_sched workbook from the Lesson 05 folder.

2. Display the **Production Schedule** worksheet.

3. Choose **File→Save As** 🗔.

4. In the Save As dialog box, choose **Single File Web Page** from the Save As Type list.

5. For the **Save** option, choose **Selection: Sheet**.

6. Click the **Change Title** button in the bottom-right corner of the Save As dialog box.

7. In the Enter Text dialog box, type `AR Production Schedule` and click **OK**.

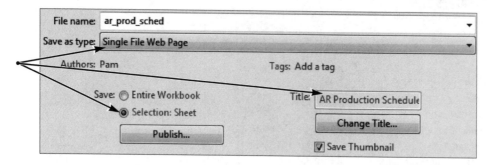

8. Click **Save**.

9. Place a checkmark next to **Open Published Web Page in Browser**.

10. Click **Publish**.

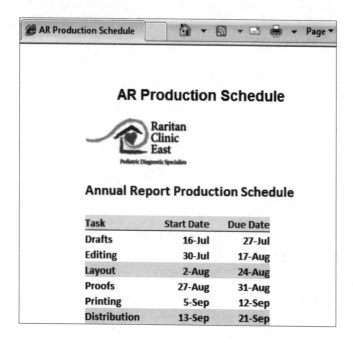

11. **Close** the browser window.

12. **Close** the workbook without saving, and **exit** Excel.

Concepts Review

Concepts Review   labyrinthelab.com/fastcourse_excel10

To check your knowledge of the key concepts introduced in this lesson, complete the Concepts Review quiz by going to the URL listed above.

Notes

Index

N

naming
  folders, 59
  macros, 18
  PivotTables, 6
native file format, 79
negative numbers, 26

O

one-variable data tables, 51
Open XML file structure, 80

P

paste functions, 91, 93
PDF file format, 85–86
personal macro workbook, 18
PivotCharts, 15–16
PivotTables
  calculations in, 13–14
  changing fields, 8–9
  creating, 3–6
  filtering in, 9–12
  formatting, 7–8
  naming, 6
  refreshing data, 14
PMT (Payment) function, 25, 26–27
position-based consolidation of data, 41, 42
positive vs. negative numbers, 26
PowerPoint, Microsoft, Excel charts in, 89–91
printing comments, 65–66
protecting documents, 74

R

records, removing duplicate, 49–50

S

Save As command, 79
Scenario Manager, 33–36
security
  Document Inspector, 66, 68–69
  macros, 17–18
  shared workbooks, 74
sharing workbooks, 69, 73–76, 88–91
Show Values As command, 13
sizing comments, 63
slicers, filtering PivotTables, 10–12
Solver, 30–33
.sparklines, 55–56
splitting data inside cells into columns, 95

styles
  PivotTable, 7, 8
  slicer, 12
SUM function, 41
Summarize Values By command, 13

T

tab delimited text files, 83
tables, data, 51–53
text file formats, 83–85, 93–94
text formatting, 63
tracked changes feature, 70–73, 74, 75
trendlines, 53–54
two-variable data tables, 51–53

U

ungrouping worksheets, 39
usernames, 63, 64, 70
user permissions, 67

V

validation of data, 43–49
values, field, 13
versions of workbooks, managing, 79–81

W

web pages, workbooks/worksheets saved as, 96–98
Word, Microsoft, and Excel data in Mail Merge, 86–88
workbooks/worksheets
  change history, 71
  converting files, 83–86
  grouping, 39–41
  marking as final, 67, 69
  merging, 73–76, 86–88
  organizing, 59–61
  PivotTables from, 6
  preparing for distribution, 66–69
  protecting, 74
  saving, 19, 20, 79–81
  sharing, 69, 73–76, 88–91
  storing macros, 18
  ungrouping, 39
  user permissions, 67
  as web pages, 96–98

X

XML file format, 80
XPS file format, 85

Notes

Notes

Notes

Notes

Notes

Notes

Notes